27 Secrets to Raising Amazing Children

27 Secrets to Raising Amazing Children

Molly Brown Koch

SIDRAN INSTITUTE PRESS
BALTIMORE, MARYLAND

Copyright 2007 Sidran Institute Press

ISBN: 1-886968-20-9
ISBN-13: 978-1886968-20-2

12 11 10 09 08 07   1   2   3   4   5

Library of Congress Cataloging-in-Publication Data

Koch, Molly Brown, 1927–
    27 secrets to raising amazing children / Molly Brown Koch.
    p.   cm.
Includes biliographical references.
    ISBN 978-1-886968-20-2 (alk. paper)
    1. Child rearing—Handbooks, manuals, etc.   2. Parenting—Handbooks, manuals, etc.   I. Title
    HQ769.K5563 2007
    649'.1—dc22   2007033552

To the late Marguerite Nussbaum,
my teacher, my mentor, my best friend,

and to the late Abraham Abramovitz,
the wisest man I ever met.

Contents

CONTENTS

Acknowledgments

I am indebted to every parent, in and out of groups, whose shared experiences, thoughts, and feelings have given me extraordinary insights into the human condition. I am deeply grateful for the lessons I learned from my children, Jessica, Andrea, and Richard, and my grandchildren, Sam, Ben, and Sara, my many students, former cult-members, and their parents. I thank Sister Margi Savage for arranging for me to share the ideas in my book with the women of Marian House III.

Plunging into the world of computers left me dazed and struggling. Mark Langrehr of Pikesville Office Supply in Baltimore saved my manuscript, and my sanity. Robyne Schroeder put the final touch on the formatting, about which I knew nothing.

I am most grateful to the people who read the manuscript and encouraged me throughout the writing of this book. Erica B. Byrne, LCSW-C, Marion Decker, Wendy Ginsburg, MS, Dorothy Katzenstein, Ann Kirby, Ellen Krieger, LCSW-C, Sandra Laken, Larry Levey, Esq., Carolyn Rodis, JD, Miriam Lowenbraun, and my daughter Jessie, who encouraged me every inch of the way. And special thanks to my manuscript editor, Barbara Lamb, who added just enough polish to make my words shine. I am ever thankful to my husband, Bill, who was always, patiently, at my side.

Your children are not your children
They are the sons and daughters of Life's longing for itself.
They come through you but not from you,
And though they are with you yet they belong not to you.

You may give them your love but not your thoughts,
For they have their own thoughts.
You may house their bodies but not their souls,
For their souls dwell in the house of tomorrow,
which you cannot visit, not even in your dreams.
You may strive to be like them,
but seek not to make them like you.
For life goes not backward nor tarries with yesterday.

You are the bows from which your children
as living arrows are sent forth
The archer sees the mark upon the path of the infinite,
and He bends you with His might
that His arrows may go swift and far.
Let our bending in the archer's hand be for gladness;
For even as He loves the arrow that flies,
so he loves also the bow that is stable.

Kahlil Gibran

27 Secrets to Raising Amazing Children

Introduction

The times they were a-changin' in the 1940s, especially when it came to raising children. New theories kept cropping up like mushrooms after the rain, and parent groups sprang up right along with them. Like many other first-time mothers, I went running in search of answers to the question, "How do you do the hardest job in the world?" Listening to the advice of one expert after another, we wound up totally confused by their differing opinions. For example, some said we should make our babies adapt to our schedules, even if it meant letting them cry for hours between feedings. Others, like pediatrician, guru of the day, and author of *Baby and Child Care*, Dr. Benjamin Spock, advised parents to limit their baby's crying to ten or fifteen minutes at most. My pediatrician prescribed keeping babies on a strict four-hour-and-not-a-minute-sooner routine. He even went so far as to tell mothers who could not tolerate their babies' cries to shut their bedroom doors and turn up the radio. I couldn't do it. Despite all my insecurities as a new mother, I followed my heart.

In that atmosphere of change, with experts arguing among themselves and our mothers' and grandmothers' advice too old-fashioned to consider, where could we turn? How could we figure out what was right for us and for our children? Along with thousands of other mothers all across the nation, I joined a Child Study Association parenting group. That was in 1949, when my first child was a year old. We turned to each other for support as we wended our way through the jumble of theories. Together we examined the experts' diverse opinions, trying them on and taking them off when they didn't fit our families' needs. Now we were able to evaluate opinions from our parents, grandparents, neighbors, even from the ever-present scowling critics in the supermarket who stood at the ready with their two-cents' worth as they watched our children fling their bodies to the floor for want of chocolate cookies. We felt as much pressure to conform to convention as we did to go out on a limb for progress. What to do? What to do?

Getting together with other mothers saved our lives or, at the very least, our sanity. Each time we discovered that our children had the same crazy-making behaviors, each time we felt that our families were "normal" and that we were not alone in our struggles, we felt like dancing in the streets. This got us through those difficult times. Above all, we came to realize that the support, acceptance, understanding, compassion, and respect we got from and gave to one another, especially when we acknowledged the mistakes we had made, were exactly what our children needed from us. These similarities gave us the insights we needed to build empathy with and understanding of our children.

We trained ourselves to open our minds. My friend Marion Decker compared an open mind to "an open window that lets in fresh air and light." So that's what we did. We opened wide the windows of our minds as we added fresh air to stale thinking and shed light on ideas and feelings that had us groping in the dark. We helped each other move forward, not only in our skills as parents but in our growth as persons. Sometimes we were able to rely on our own judgment, or intuition, as I did in the matter of my daughter's feeding schedule.

But many parents, bombarded day after day with the latest theories, opted to relegate their intuition to the backseat and put the experts in the driver's seat. In our groups, we learned to listen to both. We reconnected with our intuition and learned to trust our own judgment, then relied on the experts for their knowledge of child development. It was very useful to learn from them how to recognize which behaviors stemmed from our children's personalities, and which were normal stages all children go through.

Our exposure to each other's point of view helped us look at our own situations from various angles. Some mothers reported that even in the middle of a predicament at home, they would ask themselves, "Is there another way to see this?" This pause-to-think stopped us from jumping to hasty conclusions and delayed our reactions and overreactions. It helped us to see our children, or at least their behavior, with some objectivity. Seeing our children's behaviors from new angles prevented our emotions from becoming stumbling blocks to better parenting.

About 1956, I trained to conduct parent groups for the Baltimore County Board of Education Parent and Family Life Program. The following year I joined the Baltimore City Board of Education Parent Education Program. I've been listening to and learning from parents ever since.

It was clear we were all making mistakes—big ones, little ones, silly ones, serious ones. But it was also clear that we made them inadvertently. We simply didn't know that many of our well-intentioned actions could have unwanted results. We lacked the insight and foresight to prevent them. By listening to parents in and out of groups for over fifty years (off and on) I learned what could prevent inadvertent mistakes.

In 1974, moved by the despair of parents whose children had become involved in cults, I co-founded a support group for them in the Baltimore/Washington area. By teaching these parents the specific communication skills I had developed in my parenting groups, more than four hundred parents succeeded in reconnecting with their cult-involved sons and daughters—*despite their drastic differences.* These skills, included here, will benefit any parent who wants a better relationship with his and her child of any age.

Most of the mothers referred to in the book participated in one or more of the hundreds of groups I conducted. Other mothers were neighbors, relatives, friends, parents of children I taught, even strangers in the supermarket, and each one of them contributed to my understanding of what it means to be a parent. Some of the mothers in the vignettes were in my groups and others are composites of several parenting styles. Some anecdotes, though based on true stories, have been altered for clarity, to make more than one point, or to protect the identity of the parents.

The parents in my groups were not unusual people; they were just like you and me. The group experience helped us to see ourselves, evaluate ourselves, be honest with ourselves, and discover the wealth of answers that lie within us and in our children. I am passing along to you the lessons they learned from each other and that I learned from them.

Change—It's a Good Thing

Change is not easy. In fact, it's unsettling for even the most open-minded parent. And even if we were ready to change our thinking, we weren't sure we'd be able to act on it. At first it took time to absorb a new idea, and more time still to act on it. So what did it take to finally change our thinking and our methods? Courage. With the support of others, we found the courage to risk the uneasiness that comes with change. And it took humility. We learned this from a child psychiatrist who spoke at one of our meetings. He said even for the best-informed among us, parenting is always on-the-job training, or better still, a work-in-progress. With that attitude we could make every day a day of learning. But we thought that he of all people would have had all the answers to raising his own children. Imagine our surprise when he said, "Before I had children I had a lot of theories. After I had a few kids I had no theories left."

True or not, the quote was worth passing along to every group thereafter to help parents get the real meaning of his message—that humility goes a long way in parenting. It allows us to let go of ideas and methods that don't work and frees us to try new ones that might. "When you want something to change," he said, "look to change your method, not the child." Parents who insisted on clinging to ways that did not work blamed their children for the failure. Since their purpose in coming was to learn how they could change their children, they soon found our groups were not for them. In time, the rest of us learned to accept the idea that being flexible and open meant we might have to change ourselves when necessary. And when we did, we found the changes we made were as much for our own growth as they were for the children's good.

The "27 Secrets" in this book contain insights that will help you recognize actions that can turn out to be mistakes, how and why they are mistakes, how they affect children, and how you can avoid making them. I want to emphasize that the kind of mistakes we're dealing with here are errors in judgment, innocent in nature and often made when parents mean to teach life's little lessons. In no way can abuse, neglect, or molestation of children be called simple mistakes. These are crimes and should be dealt with accordingly.

But there's more to this book than helping you avoid mistakes. Much more. You will see how parents from many backgrounds were able to adapt the ideas in this book to make their relationships with their children close and honest, enjoyable and satisfying, rewarding and, above all, lasting. By combining the collective wisdom that grew out of their wide range of experiences and feelings with a new philosophy of parenting and two eye-opening definitions of respect, you will not just raise your children, you'll uplift them and, in the process, be yourself uplifted.

Dear Parent, this book cannot give you what it takes to be a good parent; you already have that. But what it *can* do is help you get in touch with the *best* that is in you—and with your best, you *will* raise amazing children. Parenting is what we do for our children, but it is only a part of who we are. After all is said and done, you may one day find, as I have, that who you are is what matters most to your children.

Getting in touch with the best that is in you comes from being aware of yourself and how your children's words and actions affect you. So take the time at the end of each chapter to reflect on *your* feelings, *your* ideas, *your* meanings, and *your* progress. It's a journey worth taking.

So what are amazing children? They are not carbon copies of their parents but rather their own unique and precious selves. They will amaze you with their natural capacity for compassion and love, for their kindness and inner strengths, for their warmth and sensitivity toward others. They will amaze you with their willingness to forgive, their ability to learn and grow and change and accept whatever life hands them. They will amaze you just because of who they are—and who they are is like no other person on earth.

~~

Respect Your Child

Respect, like a diamond, has many facets, and each facet holds a secret to raising amazing children. In this chapter, you will find new meanings and new ways to look at respect. Let's start with this idea: *If it isn't mutual, it isn't respect.*

Back in the 1950s, one parent group helped me search for a working definition of respect. We began by rejecting any definition that associated respect with attaining special status, position, or achievements. We felt that such attainments play to a society that values people more for what they *do* than for who they *are*. The meaning we sought had to reflect our respect for people. The one we found had a spiritual touch, yet it came from a word none of us would have ever associated with parenting. The word was *justice.*

A New Light on Respect

In his commentary on justice (Deut.16:20), Rabbi Doctor Joseph Hertz, the Chief Rabbi of England, said that "each human life is sacred, and of infinite worth. In consequence, a human being cannot be treated as a chattel, or a thing, but must be treated as a *personality*; and as a personality, every human being is the possessor of the right to life, honor, and the fruits of his labor.

Justice is the *awe-inspired respect for the personality of others, and their inalienable rights.*"

In these words we found our philosophy for parenting and the basis for all of the secrets to raising amazing children. Respect is the overarching secret and the first facet of respect is: *Regard each child—each personality—as sacred just as he and she comes to you.* With this as our foundation, we felt we were already standing taller, and reaching higher. Then Dr. Hertz added: "Justice is a positive conception—including every endeavor to bring out what is highest and best in others." This endeavor to bring out what is highest and best in our children became our mandate and our destination. But we needed to know how to get there. We had to find out exactly how one respects the personality of each child. What should we do to show respect? What shouldn't we do? And what is respect, after all?

Two dictionary definitions launched us on our journey. The first definition of respect is to "look again," to *re-spect*, or, more specifically for our purposes, to look again with particular attention at each child, to see each child *as* he or she is, for *who* he or she is. And we reach the highest peak of respect when we *accept* each child just *as* he or she is, for *who* he or she is and *not for what we want or need him or her to be.*

The second definition of respect is to "refrain from interfering with." Does this mean we are supposed to let our children do anything they want to do? No, not at all! There are times when we must interfere with what they do to socialize or protect them. But interfering with what they *do* is not the same as interfering with who they *are.* Can we refrain from interfering with our children's personalities and their rights and still give them the guidance and values they'll need? Of course we can. Is it a tall order? Sure, it is. Can we do it? Yes, we *can.* We'll just have to stand tall to achieve it.

Now that we had working definitions of respect, we had to figure out what rights children have that we need to respect. We came up with the following list.

All children have the right

- to be safe and secure in their homes,
- to live their own lives to the best of their ability and in accordance with their own *healthy* needs and desires,
- to express their feelings and ideas,
- to develop values they can cherish,
- to pursue their own dreams—not ours,
- to be loved and accepted,
- and above all, to be who they are and who they can become.

Respect Prevents Alienation

From my experience as a parent, grandparent, parent-educator, religious school teacher of children from ages five to sixteen for over thirty years, outreach group leader to at-risk youth from ages fourteen to nineteen, and counselor to parents of cult-involved children, I have come to believe that respect for children has the power to prevent alienation. And it can heal a breach once it has occurred. For parents, respecting children creates a bond that results in our remaining significant persons in their lives. It fosters self-respect and gives them the inner strength to resist the destructive influences in society. For those of us who are teachers, respecting children has the power to inscribe our lessons on

---

New ways to see respect:

- Regard your child's personality as sacred—safeguard and preserve it.
- See your child just as he or she is.
- Accept and respect your child for who he or she is, and not for what you want or need him or her to be.
- Refrain from interfering with who your child is.

---

their minds and hearts for years to come. And it is never too late to start.

Throughout the book, you will find true-to-life vignettes that demonstrate how respect can change potentially alienating situations into experiences that create lasting connections with your children. Though the new definitions of respect may have surprised you, you will see how easily they apply to everyday living.

SECRET 2

⌒◯

Get to Know Your Child

Dr. Maria Montessori's statement, "I studied my students and they taught me how to teach," touches on the second secret—get to know your child. Dr. Montessori's advice to teachers is just as sound for parents: As you study your children they will teach you how to parent them. How else can you know what traits and characteristics and sensitivities each child possesses? How else can you know what needs are uniquely theirs? To raise amazing children, you'll need to find out who each one is.

Have you ever wished your babies had come with an owner's manual? Well, they do! Every baby not only comes with an owner's manual, each baby *is* the owner's manual. All you have to do is learn how to "study" them. By paying attention, you will discover each child's particular needs, strengths, talents, vulnerabilities, and limitations. Bookstores are brimming with parenting books. Some offer excellent techniques on discipline; others give information about how children develop. But to know *your* child in particular, you have only to look to him and her.

My friend the late Rabbi Morris Lieberman often told this version of a story that emphasizes two essentials we need to know about our children.

Two Russian peasants went to the local tavern each night after their long day in the fields. Basking in the warmth of

11

his friendship, Boris would proclaim over and over, "Ivan, I love you. I love you, Ivan. You are my dearest friend."

Night after night, Boris would repeat his proclamations of love. Finally, Ivan decided to put Boris's love to the test.

"Boris, let me ask you a question."

"Anything, my friend, you can ask me anything," Boris responded eagerly.

"Tell me, Boris, do you know what I need?"

Puzzled, Boris snapped back, "Need? How should I know what you need? All I know is I love you, you are my dearest friend."

"Then tell me, Boris, do you know what hurts me?"

"What are you talking about? Need? Hurt? Why do you ask me such foolish questions? I told you, I love you, that's all there is to it."

"Ah, Boris, but that is *not* all there is to it. If you don't know what I need and you don't know what hurts me, how can you say you love me?"

The Double Gift of Discovery

Each time you discover a new aspect of your child's personality, you will give him or her the gift of gaining insight into him- or herself. While you listen to your children as they express their thoughts and feelings, you'll not only learn who they are, but at the same time you will give them a chance to clarify for themselves what *they* think and feel. Getting to know themselves as they grow up will prevent the kind of identity crisis that causes people to go off to distant places to "find themselves." In recent years, many people have left their homes, their families, and their careers to search for a lost self—a self lost in a maze of other people's definitions or labels or expectations. Children who grow up knowing who they are will have no need to risk life and limb by going into dangerous places or situations to "prove themselves."

By helping your children know themselves and have an appreciation for who they are, you will help them find what it takes to become who *they* were meant to be.

Consider what happens to children who grow up without a clue as to who they are. Some spend their entire lives living by other people's definitions of them, never knowing their true selves—who they are, and who they could have become. Some turn to drugs or alcohol or reckless sex to fill the void or deaden the pain of their emptiness. For others, pain and sadness turn to rage, and the rage turns to violence. And far too many teenagers, finding no relief from their despair, turn it against themselves by committing suicide.

Getting to Know Your Children

I once asked a group of parents, "How do you get to know your children?" One mother said she always asks her four-year-old son to explain his behavior. If she and her son have a history of trust and openness, if he knows he will not be censured or condemned, if he knows his parents' love is unconditional, and if he can figure out his reason for his behavior, she might get an answer from him and an insight into him. If he does not have these assurances, it's not likely she will get an honest answer. If he doesn't know the reason for his behavior, he might just shrug off the question. Or he might fabricate a reason just to give her an answer. If he does know the meaning of his behavior and the answer would make him look bad in his parents' eyes, he might resort to lying. If he's too embarrassed to tell, he might just giggle. If something he said in the past hurt his mother's feelings, he might not want to risk speaking out again. (This is one of several reasons why it is important for parents to consider the effects of their emotional reactions.)

Children want their parents to have a good opinion of them even if they have to lie to get it—and they need to have a good opinion of themselves, even if they have to lie to themselves.

Asking children to explain their behavior insinuates our disapproval. For instance, we never ask them to explain behaviors we approve of, like "Why are you doing your homework?" or "Why are you brushing your teeth?" So, take notice of the kinds of questions you ask your children about their actions and how you sound, and you might get an idea of what the child senses in your questions. In his book *A Good Enough Parent*, Dr. Bruno Bettelheim says, "I was persuaded that 'Why?' was usually asked in a critical spirit and with an a priori assumption that I could have no valid reason for what I was up to. Parents assume that 'why' is a neutral word, but children sense otherwise."

When asked to explain their behavior, sensing disapproval, children rise to their own defense. And in defending their actions, they learn nothing about themselves or their behavior. Dr. Bettelheim sums up the issue of questioning children: "If the child does not know his true motives, questioning will make him feel helpless, insecure, and uncertain in the future about the validity of his actions."

When questions don't get answers . . .

A relationship based on mutual trust and respect creates a place where your child feels safe enough to be honest with you and with him- or herself. In such an atmosphere, children are more inclined to volunteer their reasons for their behavior without your having to ask. Instead of asking questions to learn about your children or find out what they've done, try this:

- Be involved with them, observe them, listen to them with an open mind and a compassionate heart.
- When they talk to you, save your opinions, criticism, or lessons on life for another time.

But what do you do if you suspect that your child is in some kind of difficulty and you don't question him? Under these circumstances, a gentle inquiry is certainly warranted. *I have a feeling something is troubling you.* If he does not respond and he appears troubled, if his behavior or demeanor changes suddenly, if he seems to be unusually vulnerable, sensitive, irritable, different in any way, obvious or subtle, waste no time in getting help from a mental health professional. He or she would first recommend a full medical evaluation to rule out any physical problems, and then proceed to uncover what psychological, emotional, or social problems your child might be having.

One way to get to know your child is by hypothesizing. Do it alone or brainstorm with your spouse, or parent, or anyone else who has frequent opportunities to observe your child.

- Take an aspect of your child's behavior (especially one that puzzles you) and, keeping her personality in mind, explore (without censoring) possible motives or reasons she could have. Be sure to include family traits that might come into play. Then run down motives that could apply to any child. By delving into a wide range of possibilities, you might hit upon one that resonates. You will know you've uncovered a clue when your intuition kicks in and you have an *aha!* reaction to a particular idea.
- Tuck the information away in your memory (or better still, write it down) and check back with it every once in a while to see if the idea continues to fit in with your hunch.

SECRET 3

◠◡

Your Children Are Your Equals in Their Human Rights

According to Rabbi Doctor Hertz, respecting *every* human being is a matter of justice—it is right and just to consider everyone, children and adults, as equals in our shared humanity. In this context, no person is superior, none inferior. Does equality mean children should have the same privileges as adults? Certainly not. While they are equals in their basic human rights, they are not our buddies. They are not equal in experience or knowledge or judgment. According to recent research, it appears that the judgment part of adolescents' brains doesn't develop until they are young adults, so it's clear they need our guidance and teaching and mature decisions for their growth and health.

Being equals does not mean we can burden our children with the kind of adult concerns or responsibilities that will rob them of their childhood. In families where illness or financial pressures necessitate their pitching in, respect for their time, personality, needs, and capabilities will make a world of difference. A respected child would feel that her contributions to the family are greatly appreciated, especially when her parents make every effort to avoid taking advantage of her.

It is unwise for parents to make children their confidantes. Complaining to them about one's marriage, for example, not only taints their concept of marriage but could also damage their image of and possibly their relationship with the compromised parent. It could jeopardize their trust in the complaining parent as well. Gossiping about family members or friends, revealing other people's confidences, sharing secrets, or confessing past sins are too great a load for a child to carry.

The Authoritarian Parent

At a parents' meeting, a guest psychologist said parents should never give children the idea that they are equals, lest the children become unmanageable. I disagree. He emphasized that parents must have "authority," and he was right about that. There is no question that children *need* authority figures in their lives. But he failed to mention that when parents do not regard their children as equal human beings, parental authority can become damagingly authoritarian.

What, then, is the difference between the authoritative parent and the authoritarian parent? Authoritarian parents take a position of superiority. They believe that considering children as equals would undermine their parental authority. The only way to prevent their children from getting into trouble, in the present and the future, is through imposing strict rules and demanding strict obedience. They see no reason to explain their rules, they punish to enforce them or to teach a lesson, and they take the position that unquestioned obedience is a sign of respect. Some think punishment is the consequence of misbehavior. Authoritarian parents may not see that this kind of control does not generate respect, but fearfulness, and that harsh punishment will not strengthen their children but instead will make them feel powerless and unimportant.

Obedience does not equal respect. Fear of punishment or fear of losing a parent's love might get quick results, but it does not get the kind of respect proposed in this book. Moreover, while punishment may stop a behavior, it might also result in a disconnect from the punishing parent. If the punishment is harsh, the child will also disconnect from the parent who did not protect him.

Routinely dispensed harsh punishment hurts children physically, emotionally, and psychologically. It makes them angry, and angry children grow up unable to trust or respect anyone in authority—or authority of any kind, including the rules of society. It devalues them, and some children will engage in dangerous behaviors in an attempt to prove to themselves and others that they are not powerless. Others develop self-defeating defensive behaviors, repeating their mistakes over and over again, while still others seek relief from their pain by hurting themselves or others, and many more resort to drugs to anesthetize their pain or feelings of emptiness.

Authoritarian parents subscribe to the "because-I-said-so" school of parenting. By expecting their children to always "take their word for it," they run the risk of training them to submit blindly to anyone in a position of authority. Some might even reject offers of sincere help from people who are, or appear to be, in positions of authority.

Q: What is worse than a child who always obeys?

A: A child who always obeys blindly.

In a world filled with smooth talkers, whether a cult recruiter, a drug pusher, an abusive partner, a scam artist, or a sexual predator,

- How will you empower your children to question what they hear and see?

And when they express doubts or discomfort,

- How will you prepare them to feel free to question even people they trust, their teachers, clergy, neighbors, relatives—you?

Children need to have their thinking stimulated, not stifled, and parents can help them develop critical thinking skills early on. Constant demands for total obedience are hazardous to their intellectual health. Sure, many of us pull rank and say "just do it because I said so," but that's usually when there's danger to avoid or when we've run out of patience. However, thoughtful parents will take the time to explain their reasons afterward.

To Spank or Not to Spank

The battle over spanking rages on and child experts are still divided on this issue. Some insist there's nothing wrong with spanking if it's done in moderation. Others, like Dr. Laurence Steinberg, author of *The Ten Basic Principles of Good Parenting,* say that spanking does actual harm. But setting aside the question of harm, there are other considerations: Is spanking an effective way to teach? What effect will it have on your relationship with your child? Some children don't learn the lessons their parents mean to teach by spanking, and many react like victims; instead of taking personal responsibility for their actions, they simply hate the punishing parent or teacher.

Parents who spank say it does no harm if they balance spanking with love and affection. Opponents say spanking humiliates, infuriates, and may in the end foster further violence. Though parents justify spanking as the right way to prevent their children from getting into trouble, another underlying reason could be their own momentary sense of failure, resentment, frustration, anger, or helplessness. If this is what lurks beneath the surface, then this is what needs fixing. Thoughtful parents, on the other hand, will always take into consideration the effect that any form of discipline they use will have on their relationship with their children.

Questions to ask yourself about spanking:

- Do you know at what point physical punishment turns into abuse?
- Do you know your child's particular sensitivities well enough to predict how he will interpret being hit?
- Do you know whether he will be helped or hurt by being spanked?
- Will spanking make him angry? resentful? vengeful?
- Will it damage his self-image?
- Will it damage your relationship with him?
- Will your child learn from a spanking what you want to teach?
- What message does spanking send?
- Will hitting your child tell him that hitting is an acceptable way to "teach"? Will your son then "teach" his peers or younger siblings by hitting them? or later, batter his teenage girlfriend? or his wife? or his child? or anyone who disagrees with him? or a driver who cuts him off or a person who looks or sounds different or who comes from another country? Will he express his rage in violence against women or by molesting children?

Sad to say, men are no longer the only ones who resort to violence to vent their feelings; a frightening tide of female violence is also rising in America.

Labels

Children act out the words they hear and believe about themselves. This is as true of hurtful words as cherished words. All their lives, amazing children hear words of love and encouragement—words that convey their parents' faith and trust in them and in their abilities. Most of all, they hear their parents' appreciation of them just for who they are. Negative labels also brand themselves upon the child's self-image and remain there for a lifetime. Sticks and stones do break little bones, and bad names will break the spirit. And the heart.

This was Tonya's experience:

> My mother called me good-for-nothing-lazy when I was a kid. Now, no matter how much I do or how hard I work, I still think of myself in those terms. To me, good-for-nothing-lazy meant I was worthless, so I always have to be doing something. But with all my success, I still feel worthless.

These words were spoken by a successful businesswoman—a powerhouse, some called her. Despite her long hours of hard work, her poise before large audiences, and her skills, which reaped countless rewards, she could not get rid of her nagging feelings of worthlessness. Her drive to achieve came not from her desire for self-fulfillment, but from her need to overcome the negative image her mother's words had created. Some might say that her mother's words paid off by motivating Tonya to reach the top of her field. But Tonya deeply resented having been defined early on by her mother and having her life shaped by her mother's words—a life she described as not her own.

My mentor, Abe Abramovitz, used the phrase "the tyranny of benevolence" to explain that children can be made to conform through rewards of approval, affection, love, and material gain. Whether by punishment or reward, manipulating children for the purpose of changing them or imposing our will on them has the same tragic consequences: It leads them away from their unique selves. Manipulative benevolence entices them to become what *we* want them to be rather than allowing them to be who and what they are meant to be or what they choose to be. Because they enjoy the rewards, they cannot see the price they'll pay for complying through this kind of control—the loss of their individuality. Giving love, affection, and even special gifts are all right and good as long as the children understand that you are expressing your appreciation for who they are, as they are, with no strings attached, and not from any ulterior motives.

Even good labels have a downside when they are used to control or manipulate children or to change their personalities. Excessive praise puts pressure on children to live up to the level of the praise. While it is meant to motivate them or build their self-esteem, it can rebound negatively. The pressure to live up to a high standard gets so great for some children, they give up trying. Others wonder if they'd still be loved if they did not make the grade expected of them.

It's natural for people to enjoy some praise and recognition for their achievements. But parents need to be aware of the effects of giving too much praise. An overpraised child could mistakenly interpret the importance of self as self-importance. Thinking it means she is more important than others she'd miss the more respectful meaning that *every* self is important. Excessive praise can exaggerate and extenuate the child's illusion of central position, a normal condition for infants and toddlers, but inappropriate for older children, who need to learn that the world will not revolve around them forever.

When a child has mastered a skill, parents mark the occasion with a resounding "Good girl!" or "Good boy!" This sets a precedent that focuses more on the achievement than on the child's

---

Problems with excessive praise:

- If children receive excessive praise every time they perform ordinary tasks, will they expect others to be similarly impressed?
- How will the overpraised child feel when people don't react to his minor achievements as his parents did?
- Will "over-the-top" praise help children fit in and adapt to the world, or will it make them outsiders?

Children's awareness of their own abilities, bolstered by their parents' appreciation of those abilities, constitutes a truth about themselves—a truth they can trust. *Taken together, this is the stuff of self-esteem and self-confidence.* So your taking an interest in the work your children have done and in what they have learned, and acknowledging the effort they have expended, will be far more meaningful to them (and more to the point) than offering "Good girl / Good boy" platitudes. Paying such attention will verify what they already know about themselves—that they are capable.

---

intrinsic worth. It gets an early start when parents call a newborn a "good" baby because he slept through the night. There's far more to a child's goodness than the amount of time he or his parents sleep.

"Good boy / Good girl" responses continue. Toilet training, riding a bike, bringing home a school paper with an "A." Sure, we're delighted about the grade—the outcome—but that's not enough. Children need their parents to pay equal attention to the effort and skill that went into their work.

The Authoritative Parent

Now let's see if treating children as fellow human beings would undermine their parents' authority. First of all, it's a given that children need authority figures in their lives who will protect and teach them. They quite naturally accept our authority by virtue of our position as parent, our age, size, education or general knowledge, experience, and responsibilities. And we will maintain our authority in their eyes by our ongoing trustworthiness, credibility, integrity, honesty, and above all respectfulness.

Authoritative parents inspire confidence and cooperation and respect. They don't fear compromise or feel their authority is threatened by it. Children recognize their parents' right and obligation to exercise their authority. When, for example, a situation requires mature judgment, they accept that their parents have the duty to take charge, and when necessary, to suspend their rights temporarily. At the same time, the authoritative parent allows for a democratic process in some of the family decisions.

Authoritative parents welcome their children's questions. Allowing them to question you does not undermine your authority—it enhances it. You can trust that your mutually respectful relationships will stand up to their scrutiny. Authoritative parents see their children as fellow human beings, not as inferiors.

Fostering Responsibility

If spanking, labeling, and criticizing are not the best ways to stop unwanted behaviors, how can parents teach their children to take responsibility for their actions? One frustrated mother asked whether she should go to school every time her child forgot her lunch money—which happened frequently—or should she let her daughter go hungry to teach her a lesson? The first place to look for an answer is in the child's personality. Is she generally forgetful? Does she need help in organizing her life? Does she love to eat or is she more casual about eating? We find it hard to understand how a child can forget about lunch, but children have different priorities. The child who looks forward to eating will probably remember to take her money for lunch. Some parents in one group encouraged their children to remember to take their lunch boxes by letting them decide what to have for lunch and having them make it themselves. Other parents tucked special treats or funny or loving little notes in with their lunch. Letting your child go without lunch may not teach her the lesson you intend; she can probably find a way to finagle half a sandwich or money from her friends.

Here's a more effective way to help children take responsibility for themselves. Mentor them. If your child is forgetful, show her the value of making to-do lists. If she has no interest in eating, find the reason and the solution. If your son spends all of his allowance buying CDs early on, leaving him broke for the rest of the week, teach him how to budget his money. If we keep reminding ourselves that the word *discipline* means to teach, then we should be mentors, not wardens.

Creatively drawing a child's attention to her lunchbox is a kinder approach than punishing her when she forgets it. So it's a little creativity with the forgetful child and occasional special delivery for the responsible child. And most important, children need us to teach them the skills they will need for their lives—like making lists and budgeting and finding solutions to their problems.

Children learn best from the natural consequence of their acts. Help toddlers to see the connection between hitting or not sharing their toys and losing their playmates. Help older children come to grips with the reality that scanty studying leads to failing grades. And youngsters of any age can learn that the consequence of lying is to risk losing their parents' trust.

Children are capable of taking some responsibility for themselves early on. They need plenty of opportunities to make independent choices. Having the freedom to choose which dessert to have, which shirt to wear, or which game to play with gives

---

To help your children develop skill in making decisions, look for ways to develop critical thinking and prevent mindless gullibility:

- Watch age-appropriate television programs with them to raise questions and dialogue about behavior.
- Read and discuss books that deal with ways to resolve conflict.
- Make the dinner table a place to talk about the world as it is and how it could be.

---

them some control in their lives and provides them with valuable experience in decision-making.

If you are concerned with your children's ability to make wise choices, give them basic training in thinking through possible consequences. "What-if" exercises can be interesting, fun, and informative dinner conversation. Here is a time when you will learn how your children think and how they consider the outcomes of their decisions. Other children's mistaken choices or decisions can provide real-life problems to examine together and discuss.

It takes courage on our part to allow our children to make some decisions on their own. We feel confident of the outcomes when we make their decisions for them, and we feel less secure when they make them without us. Some parents in our groups thought they were teaching their children how to make decisions by making decisions for them. But that won't work unless the children are in on the process by which the parents arrive at their decisions. Still, children need their own experience in deciding for themselves.

Learning this important life skill can protect youngsters from making serious mistakes. Raised with respect, they will be willing to discuss their intentions with you. They'll be open to you when you point out the pitfalls of their choices. They'll seriously consider your views and warnings. This is how and when respect becomes mutual. However, where mutual respect and trust are missing, children may respond to parents' warnings by insisting that they "have to see for themselves," even if such seeing comes at great cost to themselves or others. Too much control is apt to stifle their curiosity, on the one hand, or make them so curious that they throw caution to the wind, on the other. Some children take rules as challenges and defy their parents in an attempt to prove that they can "take care of themselves." Many perceive their parents' control as a lack of trust.

It helps to have faith that the values your children absorbed in your family environment will guide them to make good choices. Granting them autonomy wherever and whenever it is possible

When do you allow children to decide for themselves what activities to engage in? It will help to ask yourself the following questions:

- Will the requested activity harm the child?
- Will it harm someone else?
- Will it destroy property?

If the answers to these three questions are no, and if you object to a particular activity, it is time to ask yourself these questions:

- Do you have a clear reason for objecting?
- Are you repeating the way your parents responded to your requests?
- Do your objections come out of a personal bias against the requested activity and not because there is any potential harm in it?

and safe creates a bond between parent and child. Giving them the freedom to choose and decide for themselves bespeaks our vote of confidence in them.

Whereas some children can handle criticism and take it in the constructive spirit in which it is intended, other, more sensitive children might take it as a personal rejection, reacting defensively, with hurt feelings, and learn nothing from it. Criticism enlarges self-doubt in an insecure or sensitive child. It chips away at his sense of worth and can linger in his self-image for a long time. A child's openness to criticism also depends on her relationship with her parents. A mutually trusting relationship can withstand a gentle critique without the child feeling insulted. What, then, is a healthy atmosphere for learning? Unconditional support. It gives children the freedom to self-correct. It encourages them to assess their own work, evaluate their efforts (or lack of them), and set goals for themselves. The mentor's role is one of consultant—a person who guides and inspires, a resource. A mentor believes in the child's ability to succeed.

Negative effects of criticism vs. positive effects of support

I asked a group of mothers how they would react to being told they were *not* doing a good job as parents. Sounding like a Greek chorus, they defended themselves with a resounding, "We are so!"

I then asked how they would respond to the statement, "You are doing the best job you know how to do." They answered without hesitation, "No, we're not."

When they felt attacked, they defended themselves; when they felt supported, they felt free to evaluate themselves.

SECRET 4

⌒〜

Find Common Ground

Another facet of respect is finding common ground with our children. By doing so, we communicate to them that we share in the same human dilemmas and struggles, basic needs and challenges. In the following dialogue, Anita discovers to her surprise that she and her son have the same problem.

Anita: I am really frustrated.

Donna: About?

Anita: About myself. I've learned a lot in this group, but I still don't do what I know I should.

Susan: What do you *know* you should do but don't do?

Anita: I know I shouldn't, but I still get angry with my son when he brings home poor grades when he knows he can do better.

Mary: You mean he doesn't seem to be able to do what he knows he should?

Anita: Good grief! We're both doing the same thing!

Me: Seems that way. Now let's not have all this good frustration go to waste. How do you think you can use it?

Anita: I can meet my son on common ground.

Me: Exactly! By recognizing that your son's problem is no different from your own, you can use compassion and

31

empathy to reach him instead of resorting to anger or criticism to teach him.

Meeting children on common ground enables them to identify with us and enables us to identify with them. As role models, some parents feel they must conceal their own failures and foibles. But the "perfect" parent can be awfully daunting and thereby discouraging for a child on his own bumpy road to success. We have to be willing to be fallible in their eyes. Children identify with fallibility. That's why they love the clumsy, bumbling, stumbling circus clown. But we don't have to fall on our faces to make our children feel at ease with us. We need only convey to them that as adults, no one is a finished product, and that each of us still has a way to go in our own growth process. And in that process, we're going to make mistakes.

Children watch us to learn how to deal with their mistakes. Do we make excuses for our actions or take responsibility for them? They need to observe how we strive to grow and change. They learn what it means to be a human being from the human beings around them. And learn it they will when they see people deal with their own and other people's shortcomings with compassion—people who have the capacity to understand and forgive. In a word, us.

The Perfectionist

While it is true that parents are role models, a good role model is not the same as a perfect human being. Perfectionism is a cult whose gods can never be satisfied; its creed is "nothing is ever good enough." It is a form of self-worship that demands the adoration of one's own standards. Some perfectionists work very hard at rising to their own high standards. Others demand from other people what they cannot achieve for themselves. Either way, the perfectionist's self-esteem suffers when he cannot attain perfection; it is equally hard for his child who is expected to "measure up." With no margin for error, forgiveness never enters the picture. Perfectionism is the antithesis of respect for one's humanness and rights. And it is hell to live with.

Another kind of perfectionist wants her child to be better than she is. That's what Joanna said when she was asked why she expected so much from her ten-year-old daughter, Winnie, whose demands had become so persistent that both mother and daughter reached a breaking point. Winnie felt that no matter what she did she would never be good enough to please her mother. She thought getting her mother's love depended on her succeeding in her studies. Despite her many accomplishments, she felt like a failure. When she told her mother how she felt, Joanna replied, "Then try harder." Joanna meant to motivate her child to do better, but Winnie felt only despair.

Maybe we ought to call ourselves human becomings instead of human be-ings.

A Good Role Model

What do parents mean when they say "We want our children to be better than we are?" Do they want them to make up for some lost part of their own childhood? A mother in our group who had always wanted to be a ballerina could not wait for her daughter to take dancing lessons. A father who never learned to play the piano insisted that his child take music lessons. Neither child had an interest in dancing or playing an instrument, nor did they have an aptitude for it. Sure, it's nice to have talented, well-rounded children. But we don't respect them by forcing our lost dreams on them.

The best way to inspire our children is by attending to the deficit in ourselves. We can fulfill old dreams, or create new ones, no matter how late in life. We can still learn to dance or play the

33

piano. While we busily explore our own talents, we free our children to pursue theirs. They will learn how to better themselves by observing how we improve ourselves. We will motivate them to get the most out of their lives by living our own lives fully. And as we live fully, they'll see how we handle our limitations and gifts, how we improve, grow, change, and succeed. When we fail, they'll see how we persist, how we cope with frustration, disappointment, and pain. They need to see what it takes to strive, to win, to lose, to recover, and to strive again. But a word of caution: You will defeat your purpose if you become engrossed in your own pursuits at the expense of the time you spend with your children. With scheduling and some organizing, you can pay attention to both.

In her delightful book, *Small Wonder,* Jean Grasso Fitzpatrick says that parents can offer "companionship on the journey of their children's spiritual life." We can be companions on the journey of their lives in general, and as companions, *equals.* It is only through our recognition of our children as equals—as fellow human beings—that we can achieve mutual respect and compassion.

SECRET 5

~~

Have Compassion

Compassion begins with the realization that our common humanity connects us one to another. Trying to make sense of the world around us and within us drives us all, parents and children alike. The compassionate parent sees and hears with the heart. But what does it take to develop our capacity for compassion? How do we do it?

I thought I had a fairly good understanding of compassion until I met the late Abraham Abramovitz. Abe was as extraordinary a human being as he was a psychologist. He served for thirty years as Chief of the Section on Child Development and Behavior at the Department of Health in Madison, Wisconsin, where he conducted hundreds of groups for parents and mental health professionals. Abe's distinguished career began in the late 1930s, when the First Lady of the United States, Mrs. Franklin Delano Roosevelt, envisioned an innovative institution for juvenile delinquents. Rather than confine them to the punitive environment of reform schools, as they were then called, Mrs. Roosevelt thought that it was time to find out what caused young boys to turn to crime. It was here that Abe began his lifelong effort to uncover underlying meanings of behavior, first with the boys in his charge, and by extension, any child's behavior. Abe brought an excerpt from the book *When Teachers Face Themselves,* by Arthur T. Jersild, to one of our group meetings. Here's what I learned from Abe and Mr. Jersild.

The Path to Compassion

Step One: Before you can accept your child's feelings you must first accept yourself as a whole person with a full range of emotions and feelings.

Step Two: Using your knowledge of *your* feelings enables you to accept your child's feelings.

Step Three: With acceptance and knowledge, you can ". . . embrace the child's feelings as if you were embracing an old friend with whom you shared a vital experience."

Step Four: Be willing to be tough enough to handle the impact of your child's intense emotions. When we withstand the intensity of our children's emotions, we convey to them that they need not fear their own feelings. How willing are you to face the intensity of your child's feelings? Some of us fear our children's feelings will overwhelm us or them. The impact would cause us such pain as to compel us to put an end to their feelings and our own as quickly as possible. Abe explained that being there for the raging child builds a bridge from one heart to the other—from one human being to another—making a lasting connection. But exactly how do we "accept and appreciate what the intense feelings mean to the one who experiences them"?

Step Five: Make room for compassion by removing your emotional response of fear, anger, disappointment, impatience, disapproval, or any of the other common reactions.

Step Six: ". . . and then accept and appreciate what the feelings mean to the one who experiences them"—your child.

Although we can see, or figure out, *what* a child is feeling—anger, sadness, fear, etc.—we cannot know the depth of his feeling.

How then can we accept and appreciate what the feeling means to him? Let's take as our example an angry child. At the very moment he is raging, set aside your reactions and let your *knowledge* of anger from your own experience help you accept the intensity of his anger. This puts you in the "fellowship of feeling with your child."

According to Mr. Jersild, this powerful moment lets you "know, in an emotional way, the nature of anger," and enables you to accept and appreciate what the child's feeling means to him. Here is the very essence and meaning of compassion. It is not simply a feeling for another. It is entering into the meaning and power of the emotion. We communicate compassion by not arguing with the child's feeling, trivializing it, or trying to distract him from it. The way we sound, the way we look, and the words we use will reach the child as you will see in the following scenario.

How Compassion Transforms

The following vignette illustrates Diane's frustration with her two-year-old son's behavior when she left him at daycare each morning.

Teddy is driving me nuts. We battle every morning. When I drop him off at daycare, he clings to my legs and won't let me go. I tell him I have to get to work, and I tell him how sorry I am that I have to leave him, but it doesn't help. He just keeps doing it.

Diane's days start with anger, guilt, and frustration. Her meticulous investigation of the daycare center, together with Teddy's happy mood at the end of the day, assured her that she had chosen a good and safe place for him. She needed no further assurance than the teacher's report that he usually returned to his cheerful self in just a matter of minutes after she had gone. Then what was the problem? What was Teddy trying to say?

Let's first take a practical look at Teddy. Is he the kind of child who does not adapt quickly or easily to transitions? Diane might find clues to his behavior by reviewing how he handles other departures in his life. Does he have difficulty separating only from her? Does he generally have trouble switching his emotional gears from one setting to another? Teddy reminded me of one little fellow who became our poster boy for children who are slow to adapt to transitions. In June, Stevie was still insisting on wearing his long winter corduroy pants, and in October his mother was still wrestling his summer shorts away from him. Some children just don't adapt to change as quickly as others do or as soon as we'd like them to.

Now let's take a look at what Diane communicated. Teddy picked up on her guilt. Telling him she was "sorry to leave him" was an open door for Teddy to enter. What was he to make of that? Since he has been taught to say he's sorry when he does something wrong, does he think his mom apologized because she thinks it is wrong to leave him? Children see their parents' vulnerability as an opening to start their campaign of persuasion. Pleading, then pouting (and looking pathetic, cute, or coy), then crying, then clinging, is usually the way it works. If Teddy's clinging behavior means he needs more of his mother's time, special attention at bedtime might satisfy him. In any case, by having more regard for his turmoil and less focus on his behavior, Diane would give her son the support he needs to "let go." If he needs more time and experience to realize his mom will be back at the end of the day, he could use a little reassurance each morning—"I'll be back to pick you up exactly at four o'clock."

We can't always figure out, let alone understand our children's reactions. The possibilities are endless, but one thing is certain—trying to reason with a two-year-old at the height of his emotions is an exercise in futility. Some tuned-in parents can read their children accurately. For the rest of us, it's a matter of trial and error. Yet, by looking at Teddy in the broader context of his life rather than just his morning behavior, Diane might find that her busy schedule does not allow for much special time with him. Though children's behaviors often appear the same, meanings differ for each child. We need to embrace each child's meaning.

But now, let's get back to Teddy, who is crying and clinging to his mother while she is feeling pressure to get to work on time. How can she have the kind of compassion described earlier? And what difference will it make? This time, instead of pleading or arguing with him, Diane is standing by Teddy without judging him or trying to change his feelings. Without anger or impatience, she is absorbing the full impact of his emotion. This happens because she is not overwhelmed by the force of Teddy's emotions. Her quiet acceptance sends the message that he is in a safe harbor. Now Teddy can sense his mother's support and he sees in her expression her acceptance of him. She sounds quite different now from the way she did when she was feeling angry, frustrated, and guilty. That's how the "fellowship of feeling" becomes real. Diane's compassion enables her to see Teddy's behavior in a new light. She sees that he is struggling with his feelings and that his behavior is neither uncooperative nor bad. Compassionate handling and the passage of time will bring about change in the ever-evolving child. Patience is surely a virtue here.

A Little Sympathy Goes a Long Way

Sympathy and compassion are like the chicken and the egg puzzle. Which comes first? How can you teach your children to have sympathy if they have no understanding of compassion? How can they have compassion if they have not experienced sympathy? They will learn about both each time you handle their intense emotions with compassion and sympathy. Your willingness and ability to withstand the impact of their emotions will tell them that they need not fear their feelings or be overwhelmed by them. By accepting their feelings, you are equipping them to feel for others—to have sympathy—to have compassion.

Without realizing it, some parents use words that thwart their children's developing sympathy. For example, when three-year-old Todd bruised himself, he heard "You're not hurt." His parents want to make their boy self-reliant and resilient. They want to prevent him from indulging in self-pity and they hope to teach him to take life's hard knocks in stride. They have good intentions.

Certainly children have to develop self-reliance and resiliency, and we need effective ways to teach them. But the toughen-'em-up approach may not get the results we expect. For example, Todd's mother stopped responding to his little bumps and bruises with "You're not hurt" the day she saw the debut of callousness, when Todd bopped another child on the head and he responded to the injured child's cries with "You're not hurt." Children need to experience sympathy if they are to build up their natural capacity for it. Sympathy begets sympathy. The natural sympathy they are endowed with will wither unless we help them cultivate it. If some children don't get sympathy, they'll do their childwork to get it. Interpreting lack of sympathy as a lack of love, they will go for pity. In an effort to get someone to show that they care, a child will overdramatize little injuries—or invent one. A small scrape brings about such prolonged bloodcurdling wailing that the child gets attention from the whole neighborhood as well as his parents. He's just the opposite of the brave, self-sufficient "trooper" his parents had hoped he'd be.

Sure, children can handle the hard knocks by themselves, but a little sympathy and comfort adds balm to the heart. You can see a child's need for comfort when he injures himself, then gets up, dusts himself off, and heads for home. He waits until he gets within spotting distance of his mother before he starts howling.

"You're not hurt!" sounds to a child as if his parents don't care what has happened to him. "Are you hurt?" is all it takes to show concern. If you already respond with gentle words that reflect your concern, you've no doubt noticed how it brings out the stoic, brave, "Nah, I'm okay," as your child picks himself up and goes on his way, handling his little injury without a trace of melodrama. It just takes an expression of caring for us to get what we hoped for in the first place—the absence of self-pity. Moderation is the answer—moderation that prevents us from ignoring or trivializing the child's distress on the one hand, or going overboard with pity, on the other.

The same process for building compassion applies to empathy. Children find it hard to believe us when we tell them, "I love you but I don't like what you do." They can't separate the doing from the doer. In their minds, *I do, therefore I am.* They take personally any condemnation of their behavior. They need us to respond to their person and the meaning of their behavior. We can communicate both with a simple statement: "I care about you and I care about what you do."

Your own capacity for empathy expands every time you tap into your memory for that time when you wished someone would look past your words or deeds and, without judgment or censure, simply respond to the suffering soul within you.

When comforting your children, be sure to leave room for them to nurture themselves. Say and do what will help them deal with their pain, but don't do so much that you block them from finding their own coping skills, especially the ability to nurture themselves. This is a vital inner strength they'll need when they are on their own. And whenever you demonstrate your compassion for others, make sure you let your children know that it is important for them to have compassion for themselves.

~~

Learn the Art of Listening

Listening is at the heart of the parent–child relationship—or any relationship, for that matter. In my training, I learned that good leadership, like good parenting, begins with listening. And the art of listening begins with being open to others; and being open to others requires us to set aside the most common obstacles to openness—our own opinions, moral judgments, personal feelings, and particular needs. But setting them aside does not mean we must surrender or change our opinions or feelings. Not at all. We need only suspend them temporarily so that they don't color, distort, or block out a person's message or meaning. When we are not preoccupied with our own thoughts and feelings, we clear the way to listen with our minds and with our hearts. Once done, the person speaking has our full attention. The first time I set aside my own agenda—my feelings, my arguments, and my judgments—to listen, I could see what a gift this would be to the vulnerable, unsure parents in my groups, and as a parent and teacher, a gift to my children and students as well.

Open Your Mind

Let's take a look at what many of us have unhappily encountered. Think back to a time when you were talking and the look in the listener's eyes told you she couldn't wait until you were finished so that she could talk, or she was a million miles away and not listening to you at all, or she'd rather have been talking about something else. Did it make you feel that what you were saying was not interesting or important, and by extension, that you were not interesting or important? Such inattention alienates adult or child. And it hurts.

Listening with an open mind to other adults is one thing, but you may wonder if it is possible to put aside your personal ideas and feelings while listening to your children. After all, we have a lot invested in them and there is so much at stake. Some of us do a good job of listening, that is, until another obstacle—the urge to teach—wells up in us. Feeling that we have to strike while the iron is hot, we interrupt to deliver another of life's big lessons. Of course we need to teach, but there's also a matter of timing.

Your child wants to talk to you—in itself a precious moment. So instead of seeing this as an opportunity to teach, make it a time to learn instead—a time to learn more about your child—what he or she thinks, what he or she feels, what he or she has done, who he or she is. As you will see in many of the scenarios throughout the book, there is a time to listen and a time to teach. How then can we set aside our feelings and thoughts to listen to our children as they need to be heard? Here's a story that showed me how I could be more objective.

Two teenage brothers in my outreach group came to my office, visibly upset. They told me a long, rambling story about having taken their father's rifle without his permission, then going to a friend's backyard for target practice. It ended when a bullet went through the picture window of their friend's living room and hit an expensive antique vase. They wanted me to come home with them to be a calming influence on their father when they told him what they had done. At story's end, they wanted to know why their parents couldn't be as cool, calm, and collected as I was at times like this. My obvious answer was, "You're not my kids, it's not my gun, and it's not my money."

What lesson did I learn from these boys? I recalled how I'd felt and what I was thinking at the end of their tale of woe: *Oh, you poor kids, what bad judgment you used.* This made me realize I could listen to my own children more objectively if I disconnected emotionally from them for the moment. When my children said they wanted to talk to me about a stress-inducing subject, I had by now learned how to relate to them as separate persons without all the hopes and fears and concerns I had for *my* children. There was the clue. I listened attentively to what the two teenagers had done, but because they were not my children, I did not have to worry about all the possible consequences of their actions. I was able to listen sympathetically and I could hear the sound of their remorse, and fear, and embarrassment.

- What does it take to listen to your child with an open mind? Set aside your feelings and thoughts, needs and fears, long enough to hear your child out.
- Listen as if you were listening to your neighbor's child.
- Stay emotionally neutral, subdue your urge to teach, and pay close attention.
- Listen for the details with your head and then listen with your heart for the rest of the story—the one going on inside the child.

It takes practice, but it works! (Spouses, too, appreciate such compassionate listening.)

How to Be a Compassionate Listener

Attentive listening happens when we are silent and patient. Something else I learned in training was to refrain from tagging on to a person's recitation my own ideas, opinions, feelings, or experiences. Previously, I thought adding my own story would convey support, understanding, and sympathy. But as I came to see, it doesn't necessarily work that way. However similar in nature two situations appear to be, they are not, and cannot, be the same for each person. We each bring our own special meanings, background, history, feelings, and emotions to our experiences.

An example given in training was the death of a parent. From the example, it was clear to see that a son who had a close and loving relationship with his father and a son whose relationship with his father was troubled or distant would have different reactions to the death of their father. The healthy young parent who died suddenly as the result of an accident will evoke a very different reaction than the elderly parent who had a long, painful illness. So the death of a parent is a similar situation, but it cannot be the same or have the same effect.

Though my training was geared to dialogue with adults, I found that the skills and rules I learned also apply to listening to children. For example, when your child asks whether you've had the *same* experience as hers, the rule that no two situations are the same still pertains. She may be looking for reassurances. *Am I the only one this happens to? Can I get over this? What did you do when it happened to you?* These questions surely need answers, but not at that moment. It's okay to tell her you've had an experience *like* hers, but hold back. Instead of jumping right in to share your story, reserve telling it for another time. Here's an opening to encourage your child to talk: "Yes, I did have an experience like yours, and I will be glad to tell you about it another time. But for now, I'm very interested in hearing how you feel about yours." This gives your child the space to deal with her own feelings, to sort them out, to discover her own meanings.

If she is willing to share her feelings or views, both of you will have another opportunity to get a glimpse of the inner child. Your quiet, compassionate listening gives her a chance to give voice to her own meanings. By talking it out, she sorts it out, clarifying for herself what the experience means to her. Then you may find, as have I on many occasions, that her search for meaning causes you to examine and reexamine your own meanings. This kind of listening makes each of us, adults and children, valuable catalysts for one another's growth.

Some parents, certain that any moment ought to be a chance to teach, do not think that being silent "does anything." Ah, but it does. Silence grants the other person, child or adult, the freedom to do with his or her moment of time what *he* or *she* needs to do, say what *he* or *she* needs to say, and feel or be what *he* or *she* needs to feel or be. It takes control on our part to resist the temptation to add on. But if our children need anything from us at that time, it's not our story. What they would most welcome is our patient listening and sincere interest in them.

The Chinese characters that make up the verb *listen* represent the eye, the ear, and the heart. What does this tell us about this skill? It says that we need to pay attention to the spoken word with our ears; with our eyes look for messages on the face, in the

Ear

Eyes

Undivided
attention

Heart

The Chinese characters that make up the verb "to listen" tell us something significant about this skill.

hands, and in the body language; and with our hearts, embrace the whole. Compassionate and attentive listening is an act of generosity and of grace; it is respect of the highest kind.

Another point to consider is how we respond to what we hear. A strong emotional reaction has a negative effect on children; it scares them off. They come to us, uncertain and at times fearful, to tell us what is on their minds and in their hearts. If they have experienced overreactions in the past, they might not want to risk upsetting us the next time they need to talk. Then they will retreat to an awful and lonely place, concealing themselves from us. It's a disconnect.

Saying that you know how your child feels could stifle his self-expression instead of providing the support you mean to give. Why should he bother talking it out if you already know his feelings? (A father told me he thinks boys need more encouragement to talk than girls, who are more willing to express their feelings.) So what you can do that will be of most value, to your child and to you, is to listen patiently. As you listen, you will learn just what meaning the experience has for this particular child and what struggles and worries he or she is trying to cope with.

These skills enable us to listen, not only to others, but to ourselves, to the words we speak, and to the silent voices of the internal dialogues we constantly hold with ourselves. Above all, compassionate listening trains us to hear with our hearts. After all is said and done, isn't being heard what all children really want? Aren't they, like us, yearning for someone just to be there for them when they need to pour out their hearts?

Talk about listening with the heart! Here is a wonderful true story about my immigrant grandmother, who taught me a great lesson, though she couldn't have known it. Many mothers in my groups tried her "technique" and they loved it.

Every spring of my childhood, my family drove from New York to Philadelphia to visit our grandparents to celebrate the New Year holiday with them. Since my immigrant grandmother spoke only a little English, we never knew how much she understood when we spoke to her. But this didn't stop my sister and me from running to her whenever we had a fight. First one of us, then the other would spin our long-winded, suffering side of the story to her. She always struck the same listening pose—her left hand placed on the side of her face, the fingers of her right hand spread wide and flat against her chest, her lips sucked in and pressed together, her brows knitted together by a deep frown, and all the while her head tilted from side to side rhythmically as she listened to the sing-song sound of our seemingly sad story. Maybe it was the cathartic effect of letting out a slew of grievances, old and new, or maybe my grandmother conveyed sympathy, but whatever it was we always came away feeling that she cared deeply for our suffering. Somehow, it made us feel cared about. And she did it without ever uttering a single word! Try it!

When listening to children, try this:

- Avoid interrupting, which can discourage children from continuing. They have a short attention span, and interruptions interfere with their flow of thought. And it is neither polite nor respectful.
- Resist making your child's story a mere springboard for your own story. You risk making him feel that his story is less important, especially if yours is more serious, or funnier, or sadder. Such competition, which could inhibit him from coming to talk with you in the future, is likely to leave him feeling frustrated, maybe angry, but always isolated.
- Remember that saying "I know how you feel" is inauthentic. None of us can know the depth and breadth of another person's feelings; all we can know is how we felt in similar situations.

A Time to Listen, and a Time Not to Listen

Even the best of skills, like listening, can have a downside. There's a time to listen—when children need to express their feelings and thoughts—and there is a time when we need not listen to endless, self-justifying excuses and alibis. Children could easily assume that our attentive listening means we accept their rationalizations for their behavior. We want our children to take responsibility for their behavior, and the sooner the better. Yes, some excuses are legitimate, but trying to justify their unacceptable behavior is not. A fine line separates explanations from rationalizations. You will find compassion a constant theme throughout this book. But let me assure you that having compassion does not in any way diminish the need for rules and limits, morals and ethics. Neither does it mean we should ignore children's unacceptable behaviors.

How, then, can you prevent your children from indulging in wearisome excuses and alibis? Begin by noticing what they hear from the people around them. Do they hear flimsy alibis instead of apologies? If this has been a pattern in your family, and your child is repeating it, start an honesty campaign. Talk about it openly. Teach your children the difference between an explanation and an alibi. (A person explains his behavior and takes responsibility for it. A person who alibis makes an excuse for what he's done and rather than take responsibility for it puts the blame on others or on circumstances beyond his control.) Regularly pointing out these differences will eventually take hold and the child will internalize the difference. It need not be a long lecture. One mother of a five-year-old took a short, direct approach and handled the issue in one sentence. "Stevie, no more *excuses* around here, *not mine, not Dad's, and not yours.*"

~

See the Innate Goodness in Children

No one has yet fully realized the wealth of sympathy,
kindness, and generosity hidden in the soul of the child.
The effort of every true educator should be to unlock that
treasure to stimulate the child's impulses and call forth
the best and noblest tendencies.

Emma Goldman

Emma Goldman's use of the word *educator* holds another secret
to raising amazing children. The word *educate* comes from the
same root as *educe,* which means *bring out*—not put in. So when it
comes to goodness, just realize that the goodness we thought we
had to instill in our children *is already there.* They came with it.

By observing you as you engage in your acts of kindness, your
children learn how to express their own goodness. Trust that
they want to use the gifts they possess. No doubt you have seen
their innate kindness for yourself, in children even as young as
two, who responded to your pain or sadness with their automatic
hugs, sweet pats on the back, and gentle kisses. To bring out their
natural inclination to reach out, they rely on all the hugs and
kisses you give them, behaviors that show them how to do it and
how it feels.

So children learn how to express their inborn goodness by watching the people around them perform acts of charity and loving-kindness. But to make good deeds a part of their own lifestyle, children need to be on the receiving end as well as to observe them. The act of giving becomes real and doable only after they feel they have been given to. The more we give to them in the way of thoughtfulness, compassion, and respect, the more they will have to give of themselves in kind.

In the following scenario, frustration and disappointment block a mother's sympathy for her two-year-old daughter's plight. In the replay, respect transforms the incident into a moment of lasting connectedness.

Two dozen toddlers pushed their way into the play-gym as soon as the doors opened. Some scampered excitedly over the equipment and immediately began climbing and bouncing. Two boys pushed their way through the crowd, knocking down anything in their way. And some children ignored the apparatus altogether. Once inside, two tykes stood perfectly still, staring at one another. Two little girls walked in with both caution and curiosity, and one little girl got up on her tiptoes, as if she were stepping into a secret.

Each child took to the new surroundings according to his or her own timetable of readiness, interest, and in his or her own style. Two-year-old Amanda moved backward toward the door, crying. Her mother, Letty, was puzzled and annoyed.

Letty: Amanda, come on and play!

Amanda: No.

Letty: Look! All the other children are playing!

Amanda: No!

Letty (Pushing the little girl toward the equipment): See, doesn't this look like fun?

Amanda (crying louder now): No! No! No!

Letty (now angrily): Stop crying! Nobody else is crying. Here, play with the ball. You like that.

Amanda (screaming): *NO! NO! NO!*

Letty: What in the world is the matter with you? If you don't stop crying right now, we'll go home and you won't go out for the rest of the day.

Amanda's behavior took her mother by surprise. Letty was certain her little girl would take to this new activity with her customary enthusiasm. Just when she thought she knew her child, she saw a little stranger. What made Amanda cry? Who knows? Maybe she needed more time than the others to adapt to the new experience; maybe the two pushy boys scared her; maybe she was having an off day, when her energy and endurance were low. Maybe she felt pressured to keep up with all the other children. Maybe she was worried about living up to her mother's or the play-lady's expectations. Maybe the other children's enthusiasm intimidated her; maybe she cried because she wished with all her heart that she could climb and run and bounce with the rest of them. In the last case, she certainly didn't need to hear her mother insinuate that there was something wrong with her if she didn't participate.

Different energies, different moods, different feelings—what the child ate that day, how she slept the night before, how her parents related to each other or to her at breakfast—are a few more possible factors that will affect children's responses to the world around them. New situations and new people can be scary. I put forth these possibilities to show the range of causes that might make a young child cry.

During a discussion of this scenario, a mother in the group brought out an important point the rest of us nearly missed. She told us she always feels uncomfortable with strangers at first and needs time to "warm up to them." We had no idea she ever felt ill at ease with us. But we were grateful to her for raising an issue that we need to bear in mind. Nobody is one-dimensional! She made us aware of how unrealistic it is to expect our children to behave the same way in all situations—as if they have only one predictable facet to their personality. They have the same mishmash of opposites and contradictions as the rest of us.

Amanda's unexpected behavior left Letty with numerous feelings:

- embarrassment *(Nobody else is crying)*
- frustration *(I can barely afford the time and money this program costs)*
- disappointment *(I wanted so much for Amanda to have a good time, make new friends, learn new skills)*
- resentment *(Why can't she appreciate everything I do for her?)*

Letty's good intentions and hopes evaporated in the heat of her negative feelings.

Here's a replay of the scene with the addition of respect: Amanda is crying and Letty says (with a reassuring hug), "If you'd like to, I think it will be quite all right for us to just sit here and watch."

This time Letty puts all of her personal wants and needs on hold and responds to Amanda with her heart. She sees nothing more and nothing less than a little girl in distress. Her acceptance of her daughter *as she is* tells the little girl it is okay for her to be *who she is, as she is.* What child wouldn't be warmed by such acceptance? Such a delectable message lasts a lifetime. This kind of response, filled with kindness, compassion, and respect, can change an ordinary incident into an extraordinary moment of connectedness.

Acceptance and Trust

Trust is a huge aspect of respect. In the replay, without knowing exactly what triggered her daughter's tears, Letty *trusted her to have had a valid reason to cry.* She didn't judge her behavior or her character. Neither did she force Amanda to do something she did not want to do, or was not ready to do. She respected her right to express her feelings and avoided making her feel guilty or ashamed. This time Letty respected her child's right to act and react as her own needs dictated.

54

How many of us have the courage to accept the child who is different and stands out? How would you have handled Amanda's situation?

In *Love or Perish,* psychiatrist Smiley Blanton says that everything in nature seeks to affirm itself. Children, too. Without affirmation, they might constantly tread the waters of self-doubt and resort to extreme behaviors to "prove" themselves. Letty's compassionate response was an affirmation of Amanda.

We can't know in advance how our children will respond to new situations or what will fit their particular needs. We have to do a lot of guessing because much of parenting *is* guess work, that is, until we have studied our children enough to interpret their behavior more accurately. Letty could watch how Amanda reacts in other new situations to see how she adapts. She might take a closer look at Amanda's environment to see what makes her fearful in new situations. Would the relaxed setting of a smaller play-group suit her better? All this said, we are still just guessing with such young children. So we might as well let go of our expectations, take a wait-and-see attitude, trust that the child has a valid reason for his or her reactions, and let each situation teach us a little bit more about our children.

What mother hasn't had that perplexing moment when she doesn't know whether to encourage her child to participate in a new experience or to respect her right to say no? Easy does it. Gentle encouragement is not the same as insistence. At times we can sense what our children feel, or they send us obvious messages. At other times we draw a complete blank. How can we find out what is going on inside them? Asking them to explain their behavior is useless, especially when emotions, ours or theirs, run high. Even if she had the words, Amanda would not have been able to explain her feelings to her angry mother.

Everyone in our group agreed that asking a child, "What in

the world is the matter with you?" is a humiliating question. A certain edge in the tone of voice conveys to the child that the parent *does* think, or fear, something really *is* wrong with his or her character. In contrast, notice how you sound when you suspect your child may be ill and you want to know how he feels. When you ask, "Is something the matter with you?" your tone of voice probably conveys both concern and sympathy.

Jumping to conclusions about their behavior or their motives, then responding to our own assumptions, will, over time, alienate our children. Such responses create distance. If their reasons for their behavior differ from our assumptions, they will deeply resent being told, "I know why you did that." By presuming their motives, we miss opportunities to learn about our children. We get to know who they are by being constantly curious about them. Instead of trying to analyze them and tell them who we think they are, we will learn more about them if we listen with the heart. It's another basic way to respect them.

In the replay of the play-gym scenario, Letty taught her daughter an indelible lesson in kindness, sympathy, and compassion. Amanda took in—breathed in—absorbed an attitude, a feeling, a way of doing, a way of being. Children watch us. They put each member of the family under close surveillance to learn life's lessons. They seek constantly to learn what it means to be a human being, and how to become one.

Living with children's various behaviors, moods, and reactions, day in and day out leads us to believe that we know our children—and in most ways, we do know them. But what we may not know, and need to know, is what the behavior *means to the child.* If we assume their meanings, or attribute our own meanings to their behavior, we miss the point. *Their* point.

What Is It Like to Be a Child a-Learnin'?

To get a feel for what it's like to be in the child's watchful position, imagine yourself transported to a foreign land. You find yourself placed in a family from whom you are expected to learn how to become a member of both the family and the new society. You don't know their language, their customs, or their laws. How would you know what was expected of you? How would you know what to do? Chances are you'd study the people around you, paying particular attention to their tone of voice, facial expressions, gestures, and body language. You'd watch what they do and how they do it, and you'd do it too, without understanding why.

Children are "strangers in a strange land." Though they learn to speak our language, they have, as we all do, their own meanings—meanings that come from their unique internal dictionaries. What we say to them may be quite different from what they hear. And it isn't just what we say, but how we say it that will determine whether or not they "get it." How they learn depends largely on their relationship with their parents and teachers. They are more receptive to people they trust and respect. No matter how good or important the lesson, without trust and respect you might hear them echo or act out the words in the title of Herbert Kohl's excellent book *I Won't Learn from You.*

And speaking of learning, children are not the only strangers in a strange land. Because each child comes to us a mystery, we too, are strangers in the strange land of parenting. Each child is unique, each has his or her own special needs, each one requires individual handling. We'll have more empathy for our children's struggle to adapt to the world around them when we acknowledge that we are learners here ourselves.

Children imitate the behaviors they see in their parents just as we would imitate the behavior of the people in our new foreign family. But what traits will each child choose to emulate? What determines whether your child will absorb or reject a given style or habit? If children all merely parroted what their parents do, we'd expect every child in every family to act exactly like his or her parents. We don't know what a child will take on, and neither can we know what particular aspect of ourselves will rub off on them. Each child reacts to parents in his or her own special way and each parent reacts in his or her own way to each child. Try as we might to be even-handed and fair, any number of factors can block us in this effort—our history, our emotions, the chemistry between us and a particular child, or our personal biases. Yet, we can still get to know each child well enough to identify his or her particular sensitivities. It's only in the knowing that we can meet each child's needs.

SECRET 8

⌢〜

Remove the Obstacles to Seeing Your Children as They Are

According to psychologist Abraham Abramovitz, three major obstacles stand in the way of parents seeing their children as they are:

- having preformed ideas as to who or what their children "should" be;
- interpreting children's words and actions *literally;*
- excessive sentimentality.

A little girl asked her mother: "If I have to be like you, who will be like me?"

Preformed Ideas

Having preformed ideas of who we think our children *should* be is the first obstacle standing in the way of seeing them *as they are, for who they are.* Thinking in the "I'll-decide-who-you-should-be" mode would have us make every effort to mold and shape and change our children's personalities to fit our image. If you find yourself leaning in that direction, remind yourself that each child comes with a personality yearning to reveal itself and that your responsibility is to nurture it, not change it. In the following scenario, one mother's preformed ideas or personal needs blocked her ability to see her child for who she was.

Linda took her son and his friend, six-year-old Trudy, to a new playground across town. About a dozen children, a patchwork of colors, sizes, and ages, were busily climbing, sliding, jumping, and playing on the equipment. Trudy looked around for something to do. Rings hanging high above her head presented her first challenge. She jumped and jumped until she caught one of the rings with the tips of her fingers. Mustering all of her strength, she pushed and pushed her body and swung from side to side until she caught the other. She hung there for a moment, then dropped to the ground with a look of triumph. Trudy's next challenge came as she studied the ragtag group of children scattered about. In a matter of minutes, she organized a game of hide-and-seek. She summoned all the children and gave them their assignments: who would hide, who would seek, the bounds that were in, the bounds that were out, and a host of other rules and regulations. No one was exempt from the good times ahead!

The children's squeals of delight turned to a chorus of "Don't go, don't go" when Linda announced they had to leave. She could hardly wait to tell Trudy's mother, Helen, what she had observed.

Linda's account of Trudy's success on the rings brought a slight look of disapproval. Puzzled, Linda asked, "What's wrong?" Helen replied, "I just wish she would stop acting like a boy." (Meaning: I want her to be more feminine.) The report of Trudy's ability to turn the little band of strangers into a cohesive group of play-partners was met with another look of disappointment. This time Helen seemed embarrassed. Linda asked: "What now?" Helen said, "I just wish she wasn't so darned pushy."

Helen was sure her affection and love for Trudy mattered more than her momentary negative feelings. She did not see that she was sending mixed messages. We would be wise not to under-estimate our transparency and our children's sensitivity to us. Messages get through to them with or without our verbalizing them.

Having hopes and dreams for our children is not the same as making them extensions of ourselves or, what's worse, carbon copies—or reliving or reconstructing our lives through them. Our hopes and dreams should be consonant with the child's hopes and dreams. Helen's preformed notions of what her child should be blocked her from seeing Trudy as she is—a determined, dynamic, imaginative, and friendly organizer and leader. Luckily, Helen did get to recognize and nurture Trudy's innate qualities. Now, fifteen years later, Trudy has matured into an outstanding person, student, athlete, and leader. She has a close and loving relationship with her mother.

Here's an anecdote that demonstrates a mother's good intention to spare her child the painful experiences she suffered in her youth. Though some traits are passed on to children, others, however similar they may appear to be, are not the same. Ida dreaded the thought that her four-year-old daughter, Rosie, was suffering the kind of loneliness she had experienced as a child. When Rosie stayed away from the children in her neighborhood, Ida assumed this behavior was due to shyness, and she felt that she had to "do something" about it. Most days in the summer, Rosie sat on a rocking chair in her backyard watching the children playing all around her. Each day, when her mother told her to "go out and play," Rosie answered contentedly, "I *am* playing."

Trust your intuition, Parents, and your keen powers of observation to tell you whether your child wants or needs a little encouragement to join the crowd or is content to just sit and rock in the sun.

61

Nonverbal Communication

Since children constantly observe us, they read us far better than we read them. (After all, they have to know the precise moment when they can ask for special favors, a raise in their allowance, a sleepover party, or the right time to confess their misdeeds.) They are quick to notice even the slightest scowl, or frown, or squint, or hear muttering through clenched teeth.

Frank Brown was proud that he could control his son, Vic, with just a look. But while Frank was thinking in terms of the results he got, he did not consider that a look, a glance, a grimace, a scowl, a gnashing of teeth can inflict as much pain as an unkind word. A child's imagination can lead to the worst and wildest assumptions. Vic said he took his father's glare to mean he was not even worth talking to. While a look represented real power to Frank, it diminished Vic's sense of self-worth. Our emotions play out on our faces and can communicate our feelings as powerfully as words.

I have a lasting memory of a six-year-old girl I was about to interview for a program I was doing for a Parent-Teacher Association meeting at an elementary school many years ago. Emily stood at the doorway, waiting for me to invite her into the room. The memory is so vivid, I can repeat our exchange verbatim:

> *Me* (smiling): Good morning, Emily.
> *Emily:* Can I come in now?
> *Me:* Sure enough. Please come in.
> *Emily:* Can I sit next to you?
> *Me:* Yes, of course you can.

After the interview was over:

> *Me:* Well, Emily, it's time for you to go back to your classroom.

Emily: Can't I stay here with you?

Me: I'm afraid not. Your teacher is expecting you back by now. But why do you want to stay?

Emily: Because you smiled at me.

Me: Because I smiled at you?

Emily: People don't smile at me like you did. They always smile at my sister because she has curly hair and she's pretty.

Me: Well, Emily, I think if people are busy looking for curly hair they will miss seeing how lovely you are.

Emily giggled and we hugged and I never forgot how much a mere smile had meant to this little girl.

Excessive Sentimentality

Excessive sentimentality is another obstacle to seeing our children as they are. It is the kind of high emotionalism that pushes us over the edge of sympathy into the throes of pity. When that happens, we feel that we must rush to relieve our pain—and the child's—as quickly as possible. What's more, pity has a detrimental effect on children. Consider the face of pity. What will the child read about himself in the pitying look? *Poor, pathetic me?* And what does it convey? *I'm so worried and fearful that my poor, pathetic child is incompetent? weak? and doomed?*

Worry and fear have the same unfavorable effect on children. What does a child think of himself when his parent says, "I'm so worried about you." *I can't do anything right?* It conveys a lack of confidence in him. We don't want our fears and worries to create anxiety in our children. On the other hand, if your face reflects your faith in your child's ability to handle his problems, you are telling him that he's a "can-do" person, that you believe in him, and that he can believe in himself. A look of faith is a vote of confidence.

Literal Interpretations

By interpreting children's words or behaviors literally, we miss their underlying meanings and wind up not only responding to a wrong take on a matter but also getting unintended results. In the following scenario, a literal interpretation combined with excessive sentimentality caused a mother to misread what her child needed.

Coming out of preschool, three-year-old Hannah and her mother walked hand in hand toward their car. Without warning, a classmate came running toward Hannah, screaming, "You're a baby!" Hannah screamed back, "I am NOT a baby!" After half a dozen of these exchanges and with no end in sight, Hannah turned to her mother for help. *"You* tell her I'm not a baby." It pained Sandy to see Hannah suffer. Feeling she had to comfort, protect, and support her, Sandy picked her up, held her close, and informed the little combatant that Hannah was not a baby.

At the exact moment that Hannah was feeling helpless and hopeless, Sandy took Hannah's request for help literally and stepped right in. Unfortunately, the timing of her rescue verified Hannah's feeling of inadequacy. Sandy had no idea that her well-meant action would confirm the attacker's accusation in Hannah's mind.

What else could Sandy have done? If excessive sentimentality hadn't overwhelmed her and her literal response to Hannah's request hadn't prodded her to step right in at that precise moment, she might have seen that what Hannah really needed was some reassurance that she wasn't an abysmal failure. Sandy could have saved the day and Hannah's self-confidence by walking away with Hannah and saying, "Hannah, I think you did just fine." Imagine how Hannah would have felt had she heard these words. In such spur-of-the-moment tense situations, we need to buy a little time to think before we react.

Of course, our children's hurts hurt us, but if we remember

that children have a right to their own experiences, including some tough ones, and if we see these as opportunities that can strengthen the child's courage, the hurts won't overwhelm us. Our role is not to gloss over their bad experiences but to give them the skills to cope with them. With skills come the confidence and mettle they will need for the next trial. Our children need us to show them how to learn the valuable lessons that can come out of all of their experiences, the good and the bad. Replaying the scene at the preschool, Sandy's reassurance that she did just fine gave Hannah something to hang on to when her self-image slipped away. Later, Sandy used the incident to give meaning to values she wanted to impart. At bedtime, Hannah and Sandy reviewed the day's events.

Sandy: Do you want to talk about what happened today?
Hannah: Why did that girl call me a baby?
Sandy: What can you figure out?
Hannah: She's mean.
Sandy: Sometimes people do act mean and it does hurt us.
Hannah: And she scared me.
Sandy: It seems to me you were pretty brave.
Hannah: Yeah.

Such a simple dialogue can have long-range effects. Sandy did not yield to the temptation to condemn the other child. (Who knows when the two girls will wind up best friends?) She withheld her judgment and made a distinction between the act and the actor. Sandy's simple statement about people doing mean things and the hurt it causes is a good enough lesson for now. And she might suggest that Hannah could make the most of her characteristic sense of humor and learn how to access it in times of stress. After dealing with her negative feelings, Sandy might remind Hannah that feelings of good will are alternatives to fear. She could also point out the peaceable ways her own family uses to resolve conflicts.

65

Moral Judgments

Like excessive sentimentality, our moral judgments push us into overreactions. Once we label a behavior "bad" we feel we have to nip it in the bud before it becomes a permanent part of the child's character. Consider the following scenario.

Claire was supervising bath-time for her four-year-old son, Robby, and his two-and-a-half-year-old brother, Kenny. Without warning, Kenny leaned over and kissed Robby, who responded with a resounding "Yech!"

Kenny's crestfallen expression pulled at his mother's heartstrings. "Now, Robby," she asked, "why can't you be nice? Your little brother was just trying to show you that he loves you." To which Robby replied, "I'm always the bad guy."

Robby's comment caused Claire to wonder whether she had done the right thing by favoring Kenny. She brought the incident to our group for discussion. She was asked, "Who do you think was the injured party?" At first she seemed puzzled by the question, certain that everyone would agree it was "poor little Kenny." She saw Robby's "yech" as a clear rejection of the younger boy. Yet, she said, she wondered whether she had "read it right." Besides, she didn't know what else to do. She thought she was teaching an important lesson in interpersonal relations.

Excessive sentimentality for "poor little Kenny" pushed Claire over the edge of sympathy into the ache of pity. This, coupled with her moral judgment of Robby's response, called for an immediate lesson on civility. With less sentimentality, she might have seen the matter for what it was: one boy was feeling affectionate while the other one was not. We asked Claire to consider the effects of a more neutral response: "Kenny, Robby does not want to be kissed right now. If someone wants to kiss you when you don't want to be kissed, you can say no, too."

In this case, Claire simply commented on what she saw, then added a fair-handed suggestion. These valuable lessons disappear in the riptide of emotions. With enough time to think about it later on, she might talk more about the boys' right to privacy and their right to voice their objection to unwanted touching.

If we condemn children's behavior with moral judgments that leave them with feelings of guilt and shame, they will not learn the lesson we mean to teach. So while we do not want to moralize and demoralize, there are, nonetheless, moral values children need to learn. Put some time and distance between the situation and the teaching moment. Then give your children the opportunity to examine the effects of regrettable words and actions: the effect they have on the offended person, the effect they have on their relationship with that person, and especially the effect that such words and actions have on themselves. Help them figure out how to mend the tear in the damaged relationship, and then *let them know that it is quite all right for them to forgive themselves.*

Our group discussion also raised questions about parents getting involved at all in this kind of seemingly harmless kid-to-kid interaction. Most of the mothers said they wouldn't be able to stay silent. Others said that when their emotions are involved, they don't know what to do or say. They know they want to teach a lesson right away, but they can't always see what it is at the time. Remember, you can always set your moral judgments aside so that they do not get in the way of an appropriate response. If you cannot think of an appropriate response on the spot, remember that you can get a second chance by revisiting the issue with your child after you've had time to think it through.

What words would you use to start a dialogue?

Opening lines for a dialogue (at bedtime):

- "Robby, if we could do today over, how would you change it?"
- "Robby, I don't think I considered your feelings today."
- "Robby, I did not mean to make you feel like a bad guy today."

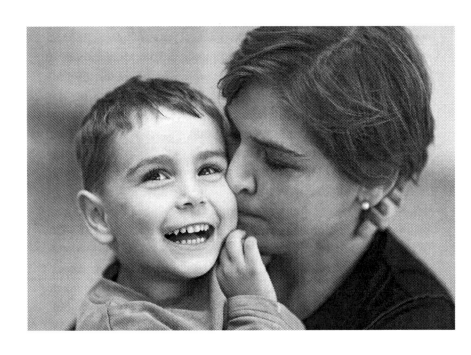

SECRET 9

~~

Pay Attention

Noted author, child expert, and educator Eda LeShan described the spoiled child as one "who gets too many of the wrong things and not enough of the right." A very right thing and an important aspect of respect is attention. Where it is lacking, a child's thrust for health urges him to fill the void and put an end to the pain he feels for having been excluded. If he feels he is not worth his parents' time, he might try to erase his sense of worthlessness by demanding more attention, more toys, more privileges.

"Demands" for Attention

Three-year-old Sidney is crying. His mother, Mimi, dismisses his crying as "just a bid for attention." She considers his demand for attention unwarranted or unimportant or both. She does not consider the need for attention to be a real need. It may be difficult to know exactly what is bothering him, but he needs his mother to trust that he *has* a reason, and he needs her to care about it. Sidney hopes his mother will stop what she is doing long enough to listen to him. A little recognition and a moment of her time may be all he needs for comfort and reassurance. What will she get across to him if she stops what she is doing long enough to find out what he wants? That he is worth her time? That he is worth-her-while? That *he* is worthwhile? But what if his mother can't stop what she is doing? If she can't accommodate him immediately, she can take notice of his need ("I see you need my attention") and tell him when she will be available ("I can't stop what I am doing now, but I will be able to give you my full attention in _____ minutes").

This much attention might be enough to satisfy him. If he persists, his mother could ask for his patience and cooperation. If that fails, she could suggest a favorite plaything until she is ready. In the end, she could at least let him know that there is nothing more she can do at that moment. Some parents are happy to drop everything and make themselves available. As long as they do not feel imposed upon, and their children are not taking advantage of them, what's the harm?

Some children who feel ignored find that their bodies will get them what they need by developing real or imagined illnesses. When that happens, we have to be careful about such selective attention. The child who gets too little attention in his everyday living, then gets tender, loving care when he is ill may associate love with illness. Thus grows the hypochondriac.

We sometimes fall into the trap of inadvertent inattention by ignoring the child who is playing quietly by herself. Let's take the case of two-year-old Bunny, who was sitting in the living room playing with her doll. She called out to her mother but got no response. She wanted a little attention. She began to bounce up and down on the sofa, calling, calling, calling. Still no response. Bunny bounced harder. Nothing. Then, when she bounced as hard as she could, with arms flailing, she knocked a picture off the wall. Her mother came rushing in (mission accomplished) and scolded her. It wasn't exactly what Bunny had hoped for, but she got her mother's attention after all. When we take notice of contented children at quiet play, they have no need to go bouncing off the wall.

In my thirty-plus years of work with cult-involved families, and with groups of at-risk youth, I met thousands of young people who had been seduced by attention in all the wrong places—by all the wrong people—cult recruiters, abusive partners, sexual predators. There are legions of disaffected youth who relieve their loneliness by medicating themselves with drugs and alcohol. The need for attention is crucial to our sense of well-being and of value. People of all ages wither without it.

Attention as a Gift of Giving

The act of giving strengthens the bond between parent and child. We don't give away something of ourselves when we give of ourselves, according to Dr. Erich Fromm in his splendid book *The Art of Loving.* Quite the contrary. The capacity to give is self-renewing. The more we give, the more we realize how much we have to give. Giving becomes easier to do and more gracious when we don't think of it as giving in or giving up.

Some parents feel that "giving in" to children encourages them to make never-ending and greater demands. The reverse is more likely to be true; children whose need for attention has been met have less reason to be demanding. Giving, however, goes both ways. We do children a disservice if we do not provide them with ample opportunities to give of themselves.

Sometimes the choreography of giving and being given to breaks down. It happens when you've run out of patience and energy and your needs collide with your children's needs. Paula, at a group meeting, bemoaned: "When I come home from work, just the thought of having to contend with my children's needs before I even get my coat off makes me hostile and angry. Before they even do anything to make me angry, I feel like screaming at them."

Who can be patient or calm or receptive when we feel stressed out or exhausted? Maybe some working parents can calm down on the ride home from work, but congested streets and aggressive drivers are not exactly conducive to winding down. If this describes you, let your children know what you need. Tell them it will make a big difference in how you will deal with them

71

afterwards. "When I come home from work I need a little time before I can do Mommy (Daddy) things again. I will be very glad to listen to you after I've washed my hands and face and changed my clothes."

Stay-at-home mothers, exhausted from the constant vigilance needed to keep young children safe all day, also feel the need for a few minutes of solitude to refresh mind, body, and spirit. For them, something like "I need a few minutes to get some new energy for the rest of the evening" might work.

These were not pleas or requests that would give the children a chance to say no. They were polite statements made with the expectation that the children will comply. It takes only a minute to explain why you need this time for yourself. Special time later with them—a walk, a talk, a few hugs on the living room sofa, a few extra moments at bedtime—will more than compensate. When we don't explain what we need and what we want, children may feel shut out and demand more and more attention. Picture it. You go into the bedroom to unwind, leaving the youngsters clamoring at the door or fighting with each other. Tensions mount on both sides of the door. Instead of feeling refreshed from a little solitude in your room, you feel guilty and angry. And though you hope they'll understand that you are trying to relax from the pressures of your job, or the day, your children feel that you are just trying to get away from them.

If you give yourself permission to recoup your mental and physical energies, recognize your need for a little space, and express it, you help both yourself and your children. While you are showing them that it's okay for you to have regard for yourself, you're teaching them that it is equally okay for them to have regard for themselves. It helps to remind them that you will respect their right to privacy when they need it. Children need this kind of honest exchange. At some other time, plan with them a number of acceptable ways to occupy themselves at those times.

We don't want to squelch our children's enthusiasm, but there are times when we can't stand at the ready to hear them out either.

We need to help them understand the importance of waiting and having consideration for others. They learn this lesson by seeing that when they control their impulses, we are able to enjoy their enthusiasm rather than resent it. Sometimes, however, our priorities and their childenergies meet head on. So, it's worth the time to discuss whose issue is more urgent at that moment, and mutually agree on which one takes priority. It's all about children learning how to be considerate, how to give, and how to respect boundaries. Teaching children to have regard for our needs is a lesson about love. When we are open about *our* needs we show them how to be open about theirs. They'll see that they can care about themselves without feeling guilty.

Each time you encourage your children to *give of themselves*, to give of their time and patience, they expand their capacity for sympathy, kindness, and generosity. Without such opportunities to express it, how will they know what goodness they possess?

Giving to Yourself

Parents who take out time for themselves to regain their emotional and physical energies find their negative feelings melt away. Their children sense the difference, and in a relaxed atmosphere they make the most of the time they spend together. They learn the satisfactions of giving in this pleasant manner. While some youngsters cooperate readily, others need more time to "get it." Patience, parents, patience. It's worth it. Just think how much you would appreciate the child who willingly gives of himself to you—his consideration, thoughtfulness, loving regard for who you are and what you need. And imagine how your child would relish the times you sacrifice your solitude to meet her more pressing needs. Mutual respect, mutual compassion, and mutual understanding reap the rewards of mutual gratitude, gracious reciprocity, and shared satisfactions. It just takes being honest about your needs.

Patty came to our group one night, angry with her teenage daughters for being insensitive to her needs.

Patty: I'm sorry I'm late.
Wendy: You seem agitated.
Patty: Agitated? I'm furious!
Wendy: What's going on?
Patty: I got home from work late, rushed through dinner, and the kids knew I had to go out—but did they offer to do the dishes for me? Noooo!
Wendy: Why didn't you ask them to do them?
Patty: Why should I *have* to ask?

Patty lamented her twin daughters' lack of consideration for her. She even wondered if they loved her if they didn't offer to pitch in and help with the dishes knowing she had to go out after a long hard day at work. She felt it was "humiliating" to have to ask. The group suggested that she discuss it with them. When she returned the following week, we eagerly awaited her report. We asked, "How did it go?" Patty answered sheepishly, "Well, I told the girls how I felt and they said, 'Why didn't you ask?' I told them I shouldn't have to ask, and they said, 'Well, Mom, since you always do the dishes, and you never ask us to do them, we didn't think of offering.'"

Patty said she realized it might have been an unrealistic expectation and told them that she would appreciate their asking if they could help sometimes. And her daughters countered, "And we'd appreciate your letting us know when you need our help." When our group examined other expectations, a mother said she not only wanted her children to do their chores without being asked, but she wanted them to do them without grumbling. Dream on, mother.

In the following confession of a "supermom," we see an unwanted and unforeseen consequence of giving people the impression that we are totally self-sufficient. Lydia said:

When I moved to this city I didn't know anyone. I felt uncomfortable asking my new neighbors for help. I figured they wouldn't need me to reciprocate since they have their own friends and family nearby. I did everything for myself. I know I gave people the impression that I didn't need anyone's help. Now that my own children are grown I see the downside of that kind of self-reliance. No matter how much they might need a hand, they won't ask for it. It never occurred to me that I was setting that kind of example.

Some parents said they were uncomfortable being on the receiving end, whether it was of time, or gifts, or even compliments. Some even deplored celebrating Mother's Day because they felt "just doing their 'job' did not warrant celebration." After we debated this issue for some time, we came to the conclusion that receiving graciously is as much a gift to the giver as the gift is to the receiver. Receiving demonstrates to children an act of generosity.

Acts of mutual giving result in feelings of gratitude, and nothing strengthens relationships more than mutual gratitude.

Embrace Reality

We have the best of all worlds when the personalities, tempos, and temperaments of both parent and child are "a good fit," as psychiatrist and author Dr. Stanley Turecki called it in *The Difficult Child*. But not all of us are lucky enough to have a naturally good fit. Some personalities clash. One low-energy mother complained that she couldn't keep up with her energetic, wriggling baby; merely holding him exhausted her and left her without the satisfactions of mothering she had hoped for. Another mother wanted to be affectionate, but her baby howled whenever she tried to hold him. She felt rejected and said it prevented her from bonding with him. Strong gender preference can put a barrier between parent and child which, if it doesn't get resolved, can remain for a lifetime. Or maybe you move fast, you talk fast, you think fast, and you get things done fast, and your child is slow moving, slow talking, and slow thinking and has trouble getting anything done on time. Or turn it around—you are the slow mover, talker, thinker, and your child is greased lightning.

Adapt to Your Child

How do you avoid nagging your child to keep up or slow down to your tempo? How do you manage to keep cool in the heat of the friction your differences create? How do you live the ordinary moments of the day when the two of you are so different? What can you do when you and your child are out of synch? The answer lies in accepting the reality of what is! Then "stretch," as they say in the theatrical world, by reaching further into your own capabilities than you have ever done before, to adapt to the child who is different. You will not only make life with your child less stressful for both of you, you'll expand your own capacity for growth, and you'll practice the utmost respect by adapting to your child instead of forcing him to adapt to you.

Parents who believe they raised all of their children the same way are at a loss to explain why one of them would reject family values and standards that their siblings readily accept. While the rules for all the children are the same, they may have a very different meaning to each child. Experts once theorized that children come into the world a blank slate upon which parents were supposed to write their life script—or create their character. This now discredited theory of the tabula rasa gave parents a free hand to use any means whatsoever to change, mold, or shape their children. This is no way to respect the child's personality.

Many of today's parents realize what grandparents have always known—that every child arrives one of a kind, each with his and her distinct talents, particular characteristics, and special traits. Grandparents accept and cherish their grandchildren whether they understand them or not.

The Child's Secret Self

Children believe their true selves are hidden within a private, secret world of feelings. They know there is a difference between the hidden self and the person who *acts* according to other people's expectations. Though they very much want us to know their inner person, they fear we won't love or accept what we see. To allow us to know them, they must first feel they can trust us and be safe with us—safe from harsh judgments, safe from criticism, safe from humiliation.

When we accept children for who they are, as they are, and we convey that we do, they are encouraged to open their private selves to us. Once they do, we have the awesome responsibility of maintaining their trust. The connection we forge through mutual trust with the revealed inner child lasts a lifetime. And when children allow themselves to venture out, revealing what is hidden within, they become *at one* with themselves, free from the strain of "hiding," free to be their whole, unfragmented selves.

Children define themselves through their actions, words, understandings, feelings, thoughts, ideas, hopes, and dreams. Rather than dictate who they must be, we need to listen as they tell us who they are and who they hope to be. Respect requires us to refrain from interfering with *their* definitions. Getting to know your children can be a wonderful adventure. It's like space travel—going to their inner space to discover the unknown. Each day gives you another opportunity to come across a new aspect of the child's personality, sparkling and new, as if you were panning for gold. Every behavior, every reaction, every mood, everything about the child reveals precious information. Just think how utterly flattered you would be to have someone at your side, caring enough to want to know all about you!

For a presentation to parents at a PTA meeting, I gathered two children from each of the grades for a panel discussion. I asked them questions like, "What is most important to you?" After the older children had given answers that included, "my mother," "my father," "my grandmother," "my bike," and "my dog," the youngest child slapped her chest and announced proudly, "Me!" After the children left the auditorium, I noticed that many of the parents in the audience were making notes. I thought they were jotting down the cute answers, so I asked them if that was true. "No," they said, they were writing down the questions to find out how their own children would have answered them.

Try this:

- Jot down some questions and write down the answers you think your child will give.
- Ask your child to answer the questions and see how close you come to his or her thoughts.
- If your child is old enough, turn the tables and have your child pose the same questions to you and guess your response.

This kind of questioning differs from grilling children about their behavior because there are no consequences here. It gives both children and parents an opportunity to learn about each other.

~

Learn How Behavior Is the Sign Language of Feelings

Four-year-old Billy was constantly on the lookout for a chance to express his feelings about the newborn interloper in the upstairs nursery. One day, he stomped on the stairs just after his mother had promised to read to him. Laura warned: "Billy, if you wake your little brother he'll be upset and cry and then I'll have to take care of him instead of reading the new book I said I would read to you." Billy stomped again. Louder.

What was Billy trying to say? Let's see if his action, coming immediately after his mother's warning, holds a clue. Did it gladden Billy's heart to hear "if you wake your little brother he will get upset and cry?" You bet it did! Making the "enemy-baby" cry would be far more satisfying than hearing a story. Billy found just the opening he needed. Stomping on the stairs gave him *an escape valve for his intense feelings.* By reducing his internal stress, he was saving his own mental health and maybe the baby's physical health as well. Abe Abramovitz called such an action a thrust for health.

Children's needs, some most urgent, are hidden in the folds of their behavior. Their messages will get through to us if our judgments don't block our view. Had Laura perceived Billy's behavior as bad, she would have felt she had to do something to prevent it from ever happening again. But sensing his behavior to be part of his struggle with his feelings about the baby softened her response. She realized that having to compete for his parents' love and attention was not a trivial matter.

Sibling Rivalry

We want our children to love each other and wish they would greet the newcomer with open arms. Many do. Many don't. A first child may find it very hard to suddenly give up being an only child. To get a feel for sibling rivalry, imagine that the law of the land changed to allow men to have more than one wife. So your husband brings home a younger, wrinkle-free, firmer in the right places, energetic new bride. She arrives at your home demanding much of your husband's attention. How would you handle the competition for his time and affection? How would you treat this interloper? What would you need from him in order to feel secure again? And what conclusion would you draw if he scolded or punished you each time you asked for his attention and reassurance?

Billy needed to know the baby had not replaced him in his mother's affection. It will take time for even an ironclad guarantee to convince him that he is still loved as he was before the baby's arrival. His mother's words needed to be reinforced with touches, hugs, smiles, compassion, and understanding. He especially needed these reassurances at the very moment of his perplexing behavior.

Laura read Billy's action with her sympathetic, compassionate heart. She did not take his action as deliberate or defiant. Instead of dealing harshly with him, she held his hands, looked into his eyes, and with a voice that came from deep within, she delivered the words he needed to hear: "Billy, we love you as much as we ever did and you are as important a member of this family as ever you were and nothing will ever change that."

Some of the mothers who discussed this matter felt these nice words would be fine had the baby stayed asleep. But what if Billy woke the baby and Laura was faced with the consequences of the baby's disrupted sleeping and feeding schedule for the rest of the day and into the night? What if it caused Laura to lose her sleep and diminished her energy and patience the next day? Some parents felt she should have punished Billy after all. Others said that punishing him would certainly not endear the baby to him. If he already felt insecure, punishing him could verify his fear that his mother loved the baby more than she loved him. Then, unhappily, Billy might vent his hurt and anger at the handiest target, the baby. At discussion's end, we agreed that the effect of the baby's interrupted sleep was a short-range and adjustable problem, whereas punishment could have long-range and not-so-easily adjusted damaging results for Billy.

The Logic of Illogical Behavior

All behavior, including yours and mine, comes out of our *inner logic*. On the surface, Billy's behavior looked irrational. If he wanted his mother's attention, wouldn't it have made more sense for him to walk the stairs quietly and have her all to himself while the baby slept? What was his inner logic? Laura's warning that he would upset the baby presented a way for Billy to get instant relief from his stress. His action was not the result of a thought process; he simply acted out his feelings. He needed to siphon off (or stomp out) his fear that the baby had replaced him in his mother's affection. We respect children when we give them the benefit of the doubt and this is what Laura did; she trusted that his action had meaning to him whether she understood it or not.

When Laura brought her story to our group some parents felt that Billy could have interpreted her hug as a reward for his "bad" behavior. Childacts do not warrant such moral judgments. Look what unintended messages he could have gotten from being punished. First, that it's a "bad" thing for him to express his feelings. Or that his mother does not understand his turmoil or care about it. Or that she really does favor his little brother. But her loving, compassionate response told him otherwise.

Later in the day, she used the stair-stomping incident to follow up with some valuable lessons. At bedtime, or some other quiet time, Laura explained to Billy that he can talk out his feelings instead of acting them out. And she assured him she would listen.

The Thrust for Health

Stomping on the stairs was Billy's thrust for health, that is to say, his attempt to keep his mental and emotional health from exploding or imploding. His action was in the language of children. On the surface, it appeared illogical. But his inner logic urged him to get what he needed—relief from the tensions the new baby generated within him. The thrust for health can take strange turns. A good symbol of it can be seen in a well-known botanical experiment. Houseplants were placed in a completely dark room. Each day a single beam of light came into the room from a different direction. The plants bent and twisted their stems to reach the light—their thrust for health. At the end of the experiment the plants were misshapen, but alive.

Children, too, will bend and twist themselves, sometimes out of shape, to reach for the light of their well-being. Billy's action brought him just what he needed—an outlet for his feelings and a reassurance of his mother's love. It makes sense when we see it from his vantage point. However, understanding that behavior comes out of an inner logic does not mean that parents should ignore unacceptable behavior. Though Laura sensed that Billy's actions gave him an outlet for his feelings and gained him an assurance of his place within the family, at an appropriate time she let him know that speaking out is a more acceptable way to express his feelings than acting them out.

SECRET 12

⁓

Respect Boundaries

Respecting boundaries often poses a dilemma for parents. It's hard to figure out when we should step in and help and when we should refrain from helping our children. Parents who say, "We bent over backward for our child," let us know how far is too far to bend. Their experiences enable us to see that too much help can compromise a child's integrity or creativity and put him on the sideline of his own life. Many of these children wind up angry, resentful, and with low self-esteem. The next vignette is a composite of several stories that illustrates how to balance our respect for our children's integrity and creativity and our duty as a helpful parent.

Instead of buying an elaborately decorated cake for her three-year-old daughter May's birthday, Karen decided to make her first-ever homemade cake. She agreed to let her older daughter, six-year-old April, stay up with her as long as she found something to do on her own.

As they settled into the warm, cozy kitchen, April sat at the table trying to think of a birthday present she could make for her little sister. She finally decided to write a story, but she needed an idea to get her started. She tried to get Karen's attention. "I'm sorry, April, but I can only do one thing at a time." April sat by quietly until, suddenly inspired, a story idea popped into her head. She wrote it down and dictated it into a tape recorder. Mother and daughter worked side by side, completely absorbed in their respective tasks. With the cake in the oven, Karen and April sat down together to listen to the tape. After all the time she had spent creating the story, writing it down, reading it through, reading it again to record it, then rewinding it, April pushed the play button to find only silence. Without a moment's hesitation she said: "I'll do it again." And she did. Karen had never seen this side of her child before. April handled her frustration and disappointment easily. The setback did not deter her; she was even good-humored about it, and determined to finish the story. Above all, she was showing tender and generous feelings toward a little sister she usually treated like a mortal enemy.

The second tape done, Karen listened to April's story about a dog and a princess—just the kind of story May would love. April wrapped it, tied it with a bow, and went to sleep. Karen finished cleaning the kitchen and headed for both girls' rooms for their nightly goodnight kiss. April was not in her own bed. Karen found both girls in May's bed, cuddled close.

Karen had a hunch that April's personal sense of satisfaction and act of generosity had spilled over into closer feelings for her little sister. Karen thought about April's creativity and the perseverance, patience, time, and effort that had gone into her project. She realized, for the first time, that April could carry through from concept to finished product on her own. The gift for May turned out to be a gift for everyone.

Karen's involvement with her cake stopped her from offering suggestions, as she usually did. Her silence freed April to turn to her own creative gifts instead of relying on her mother's. The shift from our creativity to the child's begins when we refrain from interfering, no matter how well-meaning our intentions. Paying closer attention, Karen now saw April as a generous, creative, resolute person.

When Karen told this story to our group, some parents raised questions about April's motives. One mother suggested that she might have been trying to manipulate her mother by playing the benevolent sister—using the gift idea just to stay up late. Or that she was trying to be one up on her little sister, who would have loved to stay up past her usual bedtime, too. Why make these kinds of assumptions? Why not give the child the benefit of the doubt? And anyway, what's so bad about a little girl staying up late and wanting her mommy all to herself?

When you wonder about your children's motives, stop and ask yourself:

- What good can come of negative speculations?
- Why take an adversarial position with children?
- What effect does it have on them when we suspect them of having selfish motives?

Requests for Help

How do you respond when your child asks for help? On the one hand, you may see it as your job to help. On the other hand, you may want your child to take the initiative and be creative and independent. With our advantage of age, experience, education, and exposure to the arts, we certainly have plenty of ideas to offer. But giving too many answers or ideas could have the unwanted result of short-circuiting the child's creative process. Some mothers actually do their children's art or science projects for them. This happens when parents focus more on results than on the creative process.

When a child's creativity appears to be stuck in a rut, we want to help. But how? It is safe to assume that all she needs is encouragement to get her creative juices flowing again. The following dialogue shows how it might work:

April: I have another darned school project to do.
Karen: You sound upset.

April: I am upset!
Karen: What's going on?
April: I don't know what to do.
Karen: That *is* upsetting.

Then a vote of confidence:

Karen: I'm sure you'll think of something. You always do.
April: Will you help me?
Karen: Sure, I will. I'll ask the questions, *you* come up with
the answers.

Empathy, like compassion, can work wonders. At the very least, our children will appreciate that we know and care about their feelings. Then we can help by offering stimulating questions instead of supplying answers. Since children can get easily discouraged when they hit a creative snag, they would very much appreciate hearing that it is only temporary. They will press us for answers or ideas (the easy way out for them), but what they really need is the reassurance that they're not "all washed up."

Do you see the similarity in April's and Hannah's stories? Sandy sent an unintended message when she rescued Hannah from her battle with her preschool classmate. She meant to support and comfort her child. Instead, the timing of her action verified Hannah's feeling of helplessness and inadequacy. Similarly, had Karen showered her daughter with good ideas, she not only could have stifled April's creativity but also confirmed her feeling of inadequacy.

In our meetings I noticed that parents who focus mainly on results had a tendency to give immediate answers while process-oriented parents seemed to know that the search for ideas is itself a creative act. No matter how good your idea is, the quick fix can deflate the necessary tension that creativity requires. Can you see how this kind of restraint is the greater gift to your child?

The need to allow for the tension that generates creativity reminds me of the joke about the three-year-old boy who spoke for the first time when he asked his mother to pass the salt at the dinner table. Bafflement and unbridled joy erupted over the fact that he could speak at all. After the family had settled down, his mother asked, "Why haven't you spoken before this?" In a matter-of-fact tone, he replied, "Everything was all right until now."

Autonomy—Another Way to Show Respect

In our desire to be good parents we want to make everything all right for our children, but we have to be careful that doing so does not cost them a blank spot in their originality or resourcefulness. Our children need us to stimulate their thinking more than they need us to think for them. When they are momentarily stymied, they need our *confidence* in their ability to find their own way out of it. When we trust them to think things through for themselves, they learn to believe in their own capacity to do so. Instead of giving them answers, we can still be creative in the ways we bring out their best ideas.

Children love challenges and they love solving problems. Encouraging them to exercise their ability to think critically boosts their self-esteem. One mother often posed "What if?" questions to her six-year-old twin daughters. Taking her cue from the group process, she provided them with ample opportunities to explore different ways to see situations, to figure out many solutions, and to consider a range of possible consequences, from the ridiculous to the serious. With this kind of background, they learned to think for themselves and to respect their own and each other's ideas.

Emma Goldman's idea about bringing out our children's natural gifts fits here. It tells us to bring out the child's ideas rather than put our own ideas into them. Overstepping this boundary could hinder our children from developing their imagination. It is in their best interest to send them back to their own springs of creativity rather than to have them draw upon ours. In the short run they are happy to get our answers. In the long run, however, they may regret it. If they cannot see the long-range consequences (and what youngster can?), we need to help them see. The line between helpfulness and interfering is narrow. Children need to be free to pursue and develop their talents in their own way.

Growing up in the 1930s as the child of immigrants, I was raised with old-country solutions to modern-day problems. Like most mothers of that bygone era, mine had a snappy answer and quick cure for my complaints of boredom. At the first sound of my whining about having nothing to do, my mother pointed me in the direction of the bathroom with scrub brush and bucket in hand. She delivered her orders without a shred of hesitation or guilt. Similarly, fathers led their sons to overloaded garages, cellars, or attics. Neither of my parents had the time or inclination to offer creative ideas. As it turned out, it wasn't a bad thing. With the prospect of winding up on the bathroom floor, I rarely repeated my complaint of boredom, at least not to my parents. In fact, left on my own to figure out what to do usually resulted in very imaginative play.

How Teachers Teach Tells Us How Children Learn

From the earliest possible moment in the lives of our children, we teach. We sing songs, develop our children's vocabulary, and as soon as we hear the question "Why?" we have ready answers. At some point, however, we need to add as many opportunities as possible to encourage our children to figure out things for themselves. In the introduction to her charming book, *Conversations with Children,* the late educator Edith Hunter said that the teacher's most important role is that of "midwife to thought rather than imparter of wisdom."

In the following story, Debby comes to a new understanding of the role of the teacher at both home and school when she attends an orientation meeting at her son's school.

Every day, all summer long, my five-year-old son, David, asked, "Is it September yet?" Filled with visions of new friends, books, a teacher, and his own Batman lunchbox, David could hardly wait for school to start. Finally, orientation day arrived. David was up at six o'clock, dressed in the new clothes he had laid out the night before, and was sitting at the kitchen table waiting for breakfast when I came down.

The plan was for me to accompany him into the classroom, meet the teacher, and then leave as soon he was settled in. An array of colorful posters, pictures, letters, words, numbers, and shapes covered the walls of the room. David pulled me excitedly from one thing to another, touching, looking, and asking, "What's this, Mommy, what's that?" Before I could finish answering "this," he was on to "that," and I felt increasing pressure to answer every question. When I glanced up I saw David's teacher watching us.

Mrs. Carey walked over to David, took his hand and escorted him slowly around the room. Now David was looking at each display with more discernment. When he asked, "What's this?" she replied, "What does it look like to you?" And some "What's that?"s brought, "You'll be finding out more about that in the next few weeks." I could see David's interest and enthusiasm mounting. He was not flitting from one display to another, hardly hearing the answers to his own questions, as he had done with me. He was thinking and digging for his own answers.

When I left the school, my mind was racing. At first, I wondered, "Why didn't Mrs. Carey answer all David's questions? After all, isn't that what a teacher is *supposed* to do? Isn't that what we parents always do?" When I picked up David at the end of the day he could not get his words out fast enough. A thousand disjointed sentences, phrases, words, and giggles tumbled out. I pieced them together and got a sense of what he was feeling—joy and excitement and more enthusiasm than I had seen that morning at home.

But of greater importance was that he got the point of Mrs. Carey's approach when he told me it was *his* job to learn. Mrs. Carey had already gotten across to him that they were partners in the learning process.

David's teacher showed Debby that it takes restraint, patience, and a little humility to refrain from giving quick answers. Now Debby could see the *process of learning* more clearly. Mrs. Carey worked with the children's natural drive to learn. She stimulated it by arousing their curiosity, then sustaining it. Above all, she showed respect for it. Mrs. Carey maximized David's natural wonder and interests. She knows and trusts that children have an innate desire and drive to learn.

In that brief early morning encounter, Debby saw how Mrs. Carey tapped into David's imagination and creativity. Giving quick answers appeared stifling compared to her approach. Debby could see now that teaching means encouraging children to think, to discover, to learn how to process information and make decisions. Above all else, Mrs. Carey would help the children learn how to learn and how to find their own meanings rather than merely accepting other people's answers. Understanding how children learn tells us all how to teach. They learn through their own observations, sensitivities, and interests. They learn from people they trust and admire, people they feel care about them. They learn through inspiration and affirmation. They learn from their own successes and failures. All we have to do is let them.

The brain is not a separate learning machine; feelings enter into the learning process far more than we realize. Try this:

- Hypothesize about what a child needs to be free to learn
- Make a list of the things that would hamper his or her ability to learn.

SECRET 13

⌒〜

Understand the Toddler

Two-year-olds are not "terrible," they are little messengers whose voices rise to tell us that every battle with their parents is a struggle for survival—*the survival of their identity.* They want to tell us, sometimes by screaming at the top of their lungs or by running in the opposite direction, that we have a sacred obligation to preserve their unique personalities. They speak for all children, most especially for the quiet ones of any age who cannot speak for themselves. They bring to us again and again the irrefutable message that each personality has a right to respect and the right to be loved "as is."

The two-year-old's declaration of independence begins with the word *no.* He balks at rules and in the spirit of independence. I have seen some toddlers persist in saying no even when they're offered a cookie. You can reduce the frequency of their resistance by limiting your rules to the important ones at this stage of your child's development. Less is more; the more you limit the less important demands, the more they will respond to the important ones. As a result, you will find your children becoming more receptive, and they will take you seriously. You will show respect for their drive to explore and expand their world by giving them as much autonomy as safety will allow.

Assertiveness is a positive trait and may one day be life saving. Children need their parents to work with it and nurture it, not

suppress it. Working against assertiveness, using too much control and insisting on conformity or obedience, will turn a good
characteristic into negative defiance or arbitrary stubbornness.
On the other side of the coin is the defeated child, the child who
has succumbed to the pressure to "give in" and is left depleted of
energy and spirit. It is easy to assume that a submissive child is
a cooperative child. Amazing children do not submit because
they have been worn down or made insecure; they cooperate as
respected members of their family.

Whenever a parent came to a group complaining that her child
had "a mind of her own," a voice within me always said, "keep
going, little spirit, keep going." And when I ventured to say it
aloud, we launched into a discussion about how to keep healthy
assertiveness alive.

The Little Adolescent

Two-year-olds have been called little adolescents because they
and their blossoming teenage counterparts have the same developmental work to do—assert themselves and expand their
horizons. In the past, this age group has been unfairly labeled
the Terrible Twos. But two-year-olds are not terrible; they are
reaching out, into new worlds. If we judge their enthusiasm as
rambunctiousness and their self-assertive "no" as defiance, we
will work hard to control them. Silencing their childnoise at the
expense of desirable qualities like self-assertiveness and enthusiasm is to throw the baby out with the bath water.

The two-year-old's best childwork consists of curiosity, interest,
and the drive to learn. "I'm-not-a-baby-any-more-because-I-can-
stand-on-my-own-feet-now-so-watch-out-world-here-I-come"
toddlers break out of their infant shells and make a headfirst
dash into the world to find out what it is all about. They discover
what their surroundings are made of with all of their senses.
They taste, they touch, they look and smell; they shake things to
hear them, turn things upside down and right-side up and drop

them on the floor. Everything around them is their school. Here is an experiment that will help any mother appreciate her child's need to touch. Next time you go shopping, see if you can walk through the dress aisle of the store without touching anything on the racks. Can you resist feeling with your hands what appeals to your eyes?

How do you handle toddlers who are "into everything"? What language can span autonomy, safety, and supervision without squelching curiosity or dampening their spirit? Having no words with which to ask, their touch is the childquestion, "What is this?" Before telling children "Don't touch," it helps to remember that touching is learning. One mother found the following technique worked with her sixteen-month-old boy. As he headed for an object, she anticipated him by naming it. "Oh, let's take a look at the lamp." Then, touching his arm, she demonstrated the difference between soft and hard touch before he reached for it. Walking toward another object while offering little tidbits of information to coax out their interest works very well to acquaint children with their environment.

It makes sense to put breakable objects out of reach until children are older, better coordinated, and at an age when they want to please. This is a smart thing to do, especially where there are very curious or energetic toddlers. Leaving things in place with the rationale that "children have to learn not to touch" is costly on two accounts; both the object and the child's drive to learn could get broken.

Wherever there is a potential for danger, we tend to think we have to make a big impression by issuing a strong warning in a loud voice and with a frightening look. But it could backfire. A voice louder for the stove than for the lamp could make the stove more fascinating and present a challenge to the more adventuresome child. The more fear we have, the more emotion we show, the more intriguing the object may become.

It's natural for us to feel panic at the prospect of a child injuring herself, but restraint on our part prevents us from drawing her attention to something she might otherwise ignore. Because we spend more time cooking at the stove than we do turning on the lamp, the stove may arouse more of her interest. She needs to hear "This is for mommies and daddies" in a firm, serious voice, coolly delivered. This should get the point across. We need to be careful that we don't overemphasize the dangers and thereby intrigue fearless youngsters to take it as a dare to find out for themselves. Observing your toddler as she approaches other forbidden territory will tell you if she is inclined to take risks. If she appears to be the fearless, inquisitive type, then double your efforts to monitor her closely when temptation looms. Under no circumstances and at no time should a small child be walking around in the kitchen unsupervised.

Toddlers are in a wonder-filled world of temptations. They don't understand why they can't touch the lamp or the stove. They don't have the foresight or experience to know what can go wrong: how hard a push will knock a lamp over, or what will happen if they do knock it over. They can't foresee that it may shatter if it falls and they certainly don't know how much money it cost. The sound of your loud *no* might scare the dickens out of them, but the word itself means little.

Parents assume that their children are testing them and that they "know better" when they reach for an object while looking back at their mothers. According to Dr. Alicia Lieberman, children look back at their parents for a sense of security as they venture out into the New World. Her book, *The Emotional Life of Toddlers,* explains these normal developmental behaviors and makes clear why punishments and scolding are inappropriate responses to them. The fear of being scolded or punished may enforce the limits momentarily, but fear could also curtail a child's enthusiasm to learn.

When a toddler returns repeatedly to a particular off-limits object that cannot be removed, it is easier on both the parent's and the child's nerves to distract her with something she especially likes to do. Saying no too often can frustrate a child, until she spins out of control and touches everything in sight. For those times when it is hard to reason with a child, some parents have found it helpful to have special toys in reserve. This is a hint that Kate's mother, Evelyn, could have used.

Three-year-old Kate's shrieking could be heard down the block. Her exasperated mother called me for help. The problem had started an hour earlier, when Kate wanted to watch her favorite television show, which was not scheduled to be on for several hours. The determined little girl sat in front of the television screen screaming her heart out. She was inconsolable and unremitting. Evelyn said she had "tried everything," including reading the entire television programming booklet to the near-hysterical child. At the end of an hour, Evelyn sought my help. I asked her if Kate had a special activity she enjoyed. She replied that Kate loved to play with soapsuds in the kitchen sink. As soon as Evelyn suggested it, Kate jumped up and ran into the kitchen. Perhaps she was tired of crying, or maybe this was just an offer she couldn't refuse.

We can avoid such stalemates by using a little of our imagination to capture the child's. Distraction works well at the toddler stage. Some parents worry that simply distracting children is too subtle a method and that it won't teach them what we want them to learn. In time, the toddler will be old enough to understand the limits and rules. Until then, it's easier on both you and your child to divert her attention from dangerous objects or from unreasonable demands.

Some parents reported that their more indomitable toddlers took each parental *no* as an invitation to a contest. The little tykes appeared incredulous at the idea that their parents were trying to stop them from doing what they wanted to do. Their urge to explore can be exhausting—for us, not them; but it helps to consider their frenzy of activity as a first step in their education. The world is their school without walls, and discovering it should take on the same character and feeling as reading books.

Two-year-olds are not "terrible" because they have "minds of their own," as many parents complain. They are trying on their new wings of selfhood. Like adolescents, they need to find out just what being separate and independent means. When Mommy says, "Come here," the two-year-old says, "No!" and runs in the opposite direction. Parents throw down the gauntlet when they call from a distance and demand that their toddlers come to them. It starts either a battle of wills or a game of catch-me-if-you-can. It will be much easier on your nerves to go to your child, take him by the hand, and say, "It's time to go." It's also more respectful. Saying no too often conditions toddlers to tune us out, and calling them over and over from a distance has the same unwanted consequence.

The Supermarket Battleground

The toddlers' declaration of independence turns into a war of independence when we lock horns with them in public places like the supermarket. Here even the most easygoing parent can lose control. It's not a good place to assert power over a child, who, girded by the presence of an audience, is primed for resistance at all costs. With a little planning you can avoid some battles.

Some children love to go shopping. They find the people, the sights, the sounds, and the smells of the store fascinating. Yet, those same children may not find the excursion as much fun when they are tired or hungry. And some toddlers have childenergies that can't be confined to the seat of a shopping cart under any circumstances. So what can you do when you need some things for dinner, your child is tired and cranky, you have no one to leave him with, and the hour is late? How can you show him you respect his limited endurance?

You try putting your child in the shopping cart and he screams his head off. You can't let him out of the cart or the tower of cereal boxes will come down like a house of cards. The water fountain, the soda machine, and the racks of candy beckon to him.

Can any young child leave the temptation-filled aisles of goodies untouched? Despite the pleadings and promises of "I'll be good," only the most fanatical optimist would unleash the energies of a cranky or energetic toddler into the store.

The following sentence made a lasting impression on the parents in my groups: *Always use the information you have!* Taking a young child to the store with the idea you can "control" him when you *know* even before you get there that this child "can't sit still for a minute" or that he goes nuts when he is tired is to ignore the information you have. How often do we say, "Well, I *know* she's tired, but . . ." We ask for trouble when we ignore what we know and take her anyway.

If you must take your child with you and you expect that he will be hard to manage, it is the better part of wisdom to make it a very short trip. Go for the bare essentials. Some children benefit from a little basic training, which might entail acclimating them with short trips and gradually building up to longer stays. Sometimes the promise of rewards works: "If you help me in the market I'll have time to read you two books before bedtime." Call it incentive, not bribery.

Handling a child in public places does not have to become a battle of wills, nor does taking control have to be punitive, despite the pressure brought to bear by the disapproving looks or remarks of bystanders. At these stressful times, which are difficult for both parent and child, it is still necessary to show respect for your crying child. Begin by picking him up and, in a quiet and sympathetic way, let him know you see that he is running out of patience. In the split second he quiets down (or takes a breath), tell him you how much you appreciate his waiting and that it is very helpful to you. Let him know you plan to finish your shopping as fast as you can and then you will leave. If you can make a game of rushing about, do it. If your child doesn't stop crying, give him a way to calm himself. "Take deep breaths and I will count them. Before you know it, we'll be done." (Sometimes, just counting has a calming effect.)

If the crying persists, or even gets louder, and you've reached *your* limit for patience, endurance, and benevolence, for goodness' sake, take yourself and the unhappy child home. You can't reason with a child having a tantrum once it gets going. If you've tried sympathy, empathy, and hugs, and it only gets worse, the family will just have to settle for pancakes for dinner. Does this mean you are giving in or giving up? It means neither. What you are giving is respect, understanding, and sympathy to a child whose ability to cope has come to an end.

Embarrassment over children's behavior in public places makes some parents feel they have to prove to themselves, and perhaps to the onlookers, that they still have the upper hand. They feel inadequate when they can't control the child's tantrum, and that compounds their frustration. Judging their child's behavior as "bad," their anger, like warm air, rises. Then, with people watching, they feel that they have to win the contest, if for no other reason than to save face.

If we accept that the child's behavior is the result of boredom, exhaustion, or frustration and that he has no other way to express himself as he breaks down under his internal pressure, we will have more compassion for him, and patience will follow. Children need our support and reassurance when they break down, and by giving it, we show them and the spectators what compassion and respect look like. At this point are you asking, "What about me?" Dear parents, this one *is* about you, and about reducing your stress in these difficult moments.

The Voice of Authority

Our tone of voice conveys more than the words we use. Think about the voice you use when you try to prevent a child from getting hurt. The voice that says "Stop!" as the child makes a dash for the street, for example, leaves no doubt in his mind you are serious. What is it in our tone at other times that makes children tune us out? Five-year-old Douglas had the answer to this question when his mother asked him why he listens only when she screams. He said, "I don't think you mean it when you don't yell." So how do you sound serious without screaming? An equivocal tone makes us sound unsure of ourselves, and children take that to mean the matter is negotiable. For example, what message do we send when we punctuate a directive with the question "Okay?"—as in, "It's time to go to bed now, okay?" Do you really mean to ask if it's all right with the child? If so, then you can count on the answer to be no. So, when you set limits, sound as if you mean it, and don't leave the door open for negotiation.

SECRET 14

⌒〜

Respect Childwork

It takes a lot of work to be a child. I call this effort *childwork,* and it consists of *childwords, childfeelings, childenergies, childacts.* Combining these words to form a whole symbolizes the totality of *childbeing.* The more we recognize that our children's words, feelings, and actions constitute what it is to be a child, the less inclined we will be to take personally their difficult or puzzling or hurtful behaviors. The following story illustrates how one family deals with a little girl's puzzling childwork.

Milly came to a group and asked for help with the following perplexing problem: "Our three-year-old daughter, Annie, does the strangest thing and we don't know how to stop her. Her three older sisters saw her put tiny crayon marks in the corners of the walls of their bedrooms. We don't know what it means and we don't know how to handle it."

Scolding, yelling, and punishing will stop a behavior, but merely stopping it won't tell these parents what it meant. Neither will it tell them anything about the person doing it. I suggested that Milly hold a family conference to see what they could figure out about Annie's markings. They were to use the same guidelines we used in our group—make no assumptions, look at the child in the context of the whole family, and stick to the facts, which, in this case, were:

a. Annie, youngest child in the family,
b. goes from room to room,
c. leaving tiny marks,
d. in bright colors,
e. in secret places.

The following week we anxiously awaited the outcome of Milly's family conference. Here is how they "read" Annie:

a. I, Annie, youngest of four sisters (tiny size of the marks),
b. was here (in every room).
c. I wish you could see me (bright marks but tiny),
d. but if you do, don't yell (the inconspicuous placement of the marks).

The family members looked at Annie within the family constellation. Each person questioned what role he or she played in the little girl's daily life. And they tried to understand their effect on this youngest child. Their answers held many surprises. The conference itself revealed a significant one—their realization that they were looking for a *meaning* and not a culprit. This led them to the conclusion that if there was to be change, it would have to come from *them*.

While discussing possible reasons for Annie to "leave her mark," they discovered that they each might have been taking Annie for granted. They admitted that they rarely acknowledged her presence when she came into a room. Quietly she'd come in and quietly she'd go out again. In looking for meanings, the family found their own answers. As a result, each one decided to pay more attention to Annie—to say hello, to look at her, to smile or hug her when she made her sudden appearances. Not long afterward, the marks stopped.

Milly would not say with certainty that Annie's change in behavior was due to a change in the family's response to her. The marking may have stopped because the house was being painted during that time, or because Annie had outgrown the need to do it, or because she was indeed responding to the attention she was now getting. If her behavior had persisted, the family would have gone back to their new-found method of conferring to find other possibilities. They were willing to continue looking at Annie in the context of the family instead of immediately assigning blame to her. The conference approach gave them a chance to look for underlying meanings, or messages. It brought the family members into a cohesive whole working toward changing the environment, not the child.

Just imagine how much Annie, or any child, would appreciate not being singled out, or blamed, or having the sole burden for change placed upon her. Did the family read Annie right? Milly said that, although they might never know, it didn't matter because their new attention brought the family closer and Annie seemed happier. As for Annie, she knew what she needed and she'd used childwork to communicate it.

Childwords

Some of us overreact to childwords, and we turn the child's problem into our own. Here's a picture story for you to deposit it in your memory bank and withdraw it whenever you need a reminder of *whose* problem it is.

In the first frame, a mother is standing on the shore watching her teenage daughter swim. Suddenly, a big ocean wave pulls her daughter under. In the second frame, the daughter's head reappears and with arms flailing, she cries out: *"Help! Help! Mother, I'm drowning!"* In the third frame, her mother yells back, "How can you do this to *me?"* In the fourth frame, the daughter's head is once again visible as she sputters: "This is not about *you,* Mother!"

And here is another:

Jimmy: I hate you, Mommy.
Dana: That hurts *my* feelings.

Sure, angry childwords hurt us—if we take them personally. Dana feels rejected, though at the same time she feels she's doing her duty as a proper mother by teaching her son that words can hurt. Good, Dana. It's a lesson every child must learn. But not now! This is not the time for another of life's *big* lessons. Let's see what a child does need at such a time.

Four-year-old Jimmy is expressing his authentic feeling. He needs to feel safe in his anger—safe in feeling it and safe in expressing it. He needs his mother's support and understanding and compassion. But Dana's wounded reaction put distance between herself and her son. She unintentionally switched the spotlight off Jimmy's anger and onto *her* hurt feelings. Remember Dana, this is not about you. Telling children their angry words can hurt us is not wrong. It's the timing that's off.

Now, let's put first things first. In many groups I conducted, parents expressed different feelings about anger. Some mothers said they were very uncomfortable with anger, theirs or anybody else's. They did everything they could to avoid confrontations. Other mothers felt they were being honest with themselves and others when they expressed their anger openly. "I think people ought to know exactly where I stand," one mother said. And still others admitted that, even though they feel angry, they think expressing anger will harm their children.

Now check your concept of "the happy child" to see if there is room for anger in that picture. While some parents feel that anger is harmful, others see it as a necessary and normal emotion. For parents who accept their children's right to be angry, the question is how to help them express themselves in more acceptable ways. The first rule is to wait until *after* you have dealt with the child's concerns. Stop for a moment to imagine how you would feel if you lashed out at your spouse and instead of hearing a concerned response for your distress, you heard "You hurt my feelings," followed by a lecture on how you should express yourself nicely.

The switch from Jimmy's anger to Dana's feelings left him without someone to understand, to have compassion, to care about him at that stressful moment. The message he got was that expressing his feelings is wrong, unacceptable, and hurtful to others. What is left for him to do with his anger? Bottle it up? Find another, possibly more harmful outlet for it? With no place to go with it, will he turn it against himself? Or others? And how will he deal with the guilt of hurting his mother's feelings? Dana could not foresee that her well-intentioned reaction to Jimmy's outburst had the potential to generate a slew of problems for him now and in the future.

Lastly, we need to learn how to deal with the feelings our children's anger arouses in us. We are our children's safe harbor, the place where they will be loved and accepted and understood even when, or especially when, they are angry. Child psychoanalyst Alice Miller, in *For Your Own Good*, says that "it is the inability of young children to express their rage over what has been done to them that leads to neuroses later on." It is crucial to their mental health to let their feelings out. And it is crucial to our relationship with them to accept and respect their feelings.

Take a moment to think about how you deal with anger—your own or anyone else's:

- Did you grow up learning how to deal with anger effectively?
- Were you expected to suppress your anger or were you free to express it?

Your experiences will have a profound impact on how you react to your children's anger.

When I asked parents how their children's angry childwords made them feel, one mother spoke for herself, and others agreed, when she said she felt resentful—"after all I do for that kid." "I hate you" are hardly the words of appreciation we all long to hear, but when we take a step back from our feelings they don't sound the same. They sound like what they are—childwords— the expression of honest emotions that need an outlet.

A Good Time to Teach

Bedtime, and the quiet setting of the child's room, is a good time and place to tie up the loose ends of the day's happenings. With the heat of his emotions behind him and in a calm, secure place with an attentive mother at his side, Jimmy was better able to tell her what had made him angry. It gave him and his mother a chance to clear up any misunderstandings and to offer explanations that were missed during the day. It also cleared away any lingering negative feelings to make way for positive ones. Let's see how Dana handled Jimmy's anger in the aftermath.

Dana: You were pretty mad at me today.

Jimmy takes comfort in hearing that Mom recognized what he felt. It encouraged him to talk, to consider, and to reconsider.

Jimmy: You said we would go to the park and we didn't go.
Dana: I feel bad that we couldn't go after I had promised. It got too late and we had to be home early for dinner because your dad had to go to a meeting. I know you were very disappointed and frustrated.
Jimmy: Oh, all right.

Dana put words to Jimmy's feelings to help him identify them next time. She explained why they had to change their plans and she expressed regret. Being done with negative feelings makes room for positive ones.

A word about remorse. It's good to show it, but don't overdo it. Guilt makes some parents go overboard with their apologies. Excessive apologies give children more power and guilt than they can or should have to handle. Other parents go to great lengths to try to make up for their "failures"—in this case, Dana's inability to keep her word. They buy expensive toys or plan trips or parties to compensate. Toys, trips, and parties might make the parents feel better, but they will not teach children what is essential for them to learn—that some disappointments are unavoidable and a part of life. These situations are good opportunities to teach coping skills as well as character skills, like forgiveness.

Dana could teach Jimmy to breathe deeply when he gets upset and show him how to take control of himself. Another valuable lesson for him to learn at this moment is to make the distinction between hating what people do and hating people. (We do this all the time when we say, "I love you, but I don't like what you do.") As for working off some of the energy that anger generates, give your physically active children a place to run and encourage your nonverbal children to draw pictures to vent their feelings.

How to Respond to a Child's Anger

The compassionate response would have Dana appreciate the depth and meaning of Jimmy's intense feeling. She would have entered into the "fellowship of feeling" described in the chapter on compassion (Secret Five). Then she would have acknowledged his feeling in words, "Some things make us so angry." He also needed to hear, "You have a right to your feelings, Jimmy, and you have a right to express them." If Dana's words had a calming effect, she could ask if her son could use a hug. If he was receptive, she'd embrace him, and by doing so, she would convey her acceptance of him as he is.

Such a reaction flows from a locus of love, not hurt or anger, and embraces the angry child. For the angry moment, you can just be there for the child in distress. Your support is a life raft to a child overwhelmed by the tidal wave of his own feeling. Your compassion unlocks his compassion for others. Moreover, when you show children that their feelings do not overwhelm you and that you can handle them, they get the vital message not to fear their own strong emotions; they learn that they can handle them, too. Such a gift!

Understand Childacts

What should you do when your children fight and bite and scratch, pull hair, knock each other down, hurl toys and sticks and stones? Should you intervene or leave them alone? Some child experts advise parents to let the children work out their disputes on their own. Without the prospect of bodily harm, they often do learn the limits and social rules from one another, what is acceptable and what is not. But where there is danger of real injury, few of us can stand back and do nothing. We feel that we have to protect them, body and soul. However, the time to teach civility is not during a brawl. Children can't learn anything in the heat of battle. A child so angry that he resorts to using weapons is not likely to forget it, so teaching can wait for a more receptive time. Both parents and children need cool-down time and a chance to process their feelings without assigning blame or passing judgment.

Some mothers find biting especially disturbing. Though most children outgrow this behavior fairly rapidly, some parents, feeling they cannot wait it out because of the harm it might do, hope a strong reaction of shock and condemnation will convey the seriousness of the offense. The problem is, you can't count on children to get that message. They could assume that if biting upsets you so much, it must be a really powerful weapon. Just what they wanted to know!

Several mothers in one group said they bite their children back—"to show them how it feels." Let's see if that works. If you bite softly because you really don't want to hurt your child, how will he get the point that it hurts when he does it? And if you bite him hard enough to show him that it hurts, he'll see how much pain he can inflict—which is exactly what he wants to do. Either way, soft bite or hard, he might not learn the lesson you want to teach. When parents have thought the behavior was beyond their child's control, I have recommended that they get professional help. Mental health specialists tell parents to look beyond the act of biting and look for underlying problems. Some parents found that their children lacked self-confidence or felt overwhelmed by bigger, stronger, more powerful forces in their lives. If you suspect that your child's biting is a symptom of another more serious matter, then it is that matter that needs special attention.

Time-outs

What is the purpose of a time-out? Is it meant to punish? Is it a cooling-off period? How do you determine the amount of the time to assign if the child has no concept of time? For instance, Arlene said that if Buddy's behavior did not change after a two-minute time-out, she upped the ante to five minutes. When that didn't work, she kept going until she found she was confining both of them to torturous thirty-minute periods. If the time-outs didn't bring the desired effect at the shorter period of time, what was the point of continuing?

Three-year-old Donny could not distinguish between a restorative time-out and punishment, so he found time-outs scary. His mother, Penny, had angrily warned him, "If you don't stop running around it will be time-out for you!" Donny reacted as if she had said, "It's curtains for you," because the poor little guy hid under a bed and pleaded for his very life, screaming, "No, Mommy, no!"

Here's a softer way to handle time-outs. Try a tone of kind-

Some questions to consider:

- How do children perceive a time-out?
- Have you explained its purpose?
- Have you asked your child what he or she thinks its purpose is? You might be surprised to find that the child's perception differs from your stated purpose.
- Have you asked your child how he or she feels while sitting it out? You might learn that it means too much or too little.
- Could your child take the separation from you as an act of rejection? If that is the case, consider its effect on your relationship.
- Does the time-out warning come after all pleading and bargaining have failed and you have reached your saturation point? When that happens, exasperated parents often sound angry—and scary.

---

ness when you include your own need for a time-out. "Let's take a time-out because we are both very upset and we both need to cool down and we both need to think about what happened here." This approach takes the spotlight off the child, who would feel forced to defend his behavior if he was the only one banished to his room. When the time-out is for both parent and child, neither one is the "bad guy." It also makes the child more receptive to a calm dialogue afterward.

Testing Behaviors

What mother hasn't been driven to the brink of sanity by her child's testing behaviors? Children do their best childwork when they have to find out "what will happen if . . . ?" They need to know how far they can go to find the outer limits, their parents' and their own. There are two ways to see a child's testing behaviors: as an act of defiance or as a need to find boundaries. It is interesting to note that fathers in my groups rarely complained about being pushed to the limit. My guess was their tone of voice made their rules sound unequivocal.

Toddlers will persist beyond saying no. And sometimes, when the no is loud enough, they'll make a game of it—in itself, testing a limit. Just saying no won't stop older children from pushing on, either; in fact, they just won't take no for an answer. Eddy found no reason to stop his behavior even when his mother pointed out its dire consequences.

Seven-year-old Eddy persisted in walking along the ledge of a picket fence despite his mother's pleadings to come down.

Marylou: Eddy, get down from there!
Eddy: Give me a good reason.
Marylou: You can get killed.
Eddy: That's not a good reason.

Children need to find out how far is too far, and they want to know if we will still love them no matter what they do. So they'll push us as hard and as far as they can. We need to make the limits absolutely clear so that they will know them when they see them. If we change or relax the rules one day and enforce them another, we can expect the confused child to keep testing until he finds out where the limit is.

While sitting in a doctor's waiting room, I watched a struggle between a mother and her son, who appeared to be about three. She gave him fifteen instructions (I counted) within a period of five minutes. It was apparent that the boy had tuned her out. Having nothing to do, he busied himself by climbing on the couches and jumping down. After telling him to stop time after time, she grabbed his arm and pulled him into the corridor for a time-out. They returned a few minutes later and he resumed jumping.

She told him she expected him to "act grown up," like the adults in the waiting room. She might have saved herself and the child a lot of unnecessary aggravation by bringing special toys or books to occupy him. This mother ignored the information she had about his boundless childenergy (the envy of all the rest of us in the waiting room); she ignored his short attention span and the youthful enthusiasm that sent him jumping off the furniture. Waiting is not an easy thing for a child to do. It ought to be treated like any other achievement, deserving of recognition and acknowledgment every time it happens.

How to Get Desired Results

When children do the right thing, they need to hear words of encouragement. A little boy in a restaurant illustrated the importance of this kind of attention. He repeatedly stood up to peer at the people in the adjoining booth. (Their smiles at each pop-up probably had something to do with his encore appearances.) His embarrassed mother told him to turn around and sit down. He didn't. She tried coaxing, then bribing, and after a few minutes, she threatened to spank him. He sat down, but within seconds he popped right up again. When finally he stayed down, his mother resumed her conversation with the other people at her table, saying nothing more to the little fellow.

Taking notice of him when he sat down would have given him a sense of achievement plus the bonus of his mother's appreciation. It's hard for a curious, friendly, energetic, little boy to sit down and stay down. He wants to see what's going on around him. But is the child's inquisitiveness much different from our own? Don't we also glance around to see who is dining there? The only difference is that we don't have to stand up. Words of recognition made a lasting impression on my grandson, Ben.

Three-year-old Ben begged his mother for something to eat as she was preparing his birthday luncheon. Fearing a stampede, his mother said, "Please go back into the living-room and wait. It will be just a few minutes more and then we will all have lunch."

Having heard his mother's request, I said: "Ben, are you beginning to wait already?" Ben puffed up his little chest and announced proudly, "Yes I am."

A few minutes later, I asked again, my tone suggesting that he was doing very serious and important work, "Ben, are you *still* waiting?" Stretching himself even taller, and smiling broadly, Ben again said, "Yes, I *AM!*"

At little intervals we repeated this dialogue until Ben's mother called everyone in for lunch. "My, my," I said, "that was a very grown-up thing for you to do on your third birthday." Ben, now bursting with pride, replied, "It sure was!"

To this day, Ben considers his ability to wait a major achievement. And so it is.

The Ladder of Development

I visualize the child's developmental process as a ladder—and a shaky one at that—with each rung taking each child to mysterious new heights of his or her maturation. Parents are their "handrails," providing security for them as they move upward. They test each rung, sometimes imaginatively, often haphazardly, to get their footing. Each step tells them what they have to know about themselves. How free am I? How tough am I? How big am I? What is my domain? What is yours? How much can I do on my own? How safe am I?

If any one of these questions remains unanswered at any stage, *an inner drive* will impel them to persist at the behavior until that need is met. So we tend to label children "immature" when they cling to a behavior from an earlier stage. Even as they move toward the next step of development, if they haven't mastered the last one, their emotions stay on hold and the behaviors remain on automatic replay. Each child moves forward according to his or her own timetable and personality. Some are timid and cautious; others are adventuresome and bold. Still others are resistant to change, while others find change exhilarating. Some children hold on tight to their parents for support, and others need them only in case of emergency. And then there are the fearless—those determined little characters who remain undaunted no matter what. And let's thank our lucky stars for their persistence. The child who stops trying is broken in heart and spirit. Can you describe your child's approach to growing up?

Having information about child development alleviates concern over some behaviors. It helps you distinguish between the behaviors common to all children, for example, testing behaviors, and the behaviors that stem from your child's particular personality or needs. Any of the books on child development in the bibliography will guide you through the stages.

⌒〜⌒

Control: Why You Lose It and How to Get It Back

Testing behaviors can try the souls of the most saintly among us. On good days, we can handle them better than when we are low in energy or spirits. On a bad day, testing behaviors can push us beyond our mental and physical limits. The following incident happened on the kind of day Murphy was having when he devised his Law.

Whatever could go wrong had either already gone or was on the edge. Rachel woke up with a headache, her husband was out of town, and her three-year-old daughter, Toby, was irritable and restless. They were waiting for a repairman to come and fix the heater in their freezing house. At the sound of the telephone ringing, Toby went berserk. She raced her mother to the phone, yanked it out of Rachel's hand, and ran away when it fell to the floor. Rachel's anger peaked when she picked it up and no one was at the other end. Then the repairman banged on the front door and woke the baby and the dog threw up on the living room rug.

As the man stepped inside, Toby broke down completely, crying and pulling on her mother. When Rachel threatened to spank her, Toby laughed. A warning she'd have no television for a week brought the same reaction. Rachel finally screamed, *"Stop!"* The repairman froze in his tracks while Toby continued to run circles around them both. Rachel was close to tears.

Who can stay calm on days like this, let alone figure out meanings? What parent thinks about respect at times like this? How do you get a grip on your emotions and take control of a situation when you feel you are at a complete loss?—loss of energy, loss of patience, loss of control, and loss of self-confidence. Rachel's attempts to reason with Toby failed. Feeling she had lost her own control heightened her emotions and tension. Her anger mounted toward the child who made her feel so helpless.

How to Regain Control

Try as we might to stay cool, we sometimes lash out with words and actions we later regret. Or, in an attempt to shield our children from our true feelings, we try to cover them up by *acting* calm while we seethe inside. This could make us explode—or implode—with rage at any time. The first thing parents in our group wanted to know was how to "get a grip" under such trying circumstances. Rachel's story reminded me of the game we called "Statues," which I played as a child. It went like this. One child would yell "Move" and everyone else would dance, jump, crawl, wriggle, or move excitedly one way or another. (I compared those gyrations to the out-of-control feelings of an overburdened mother.) Then the caller yelled "Freeze!" and everyone would stand perfectly still—like statues. (Whoever moved after the command was out of the game.)

With so much pressure building, Rachel needs to "freeze," to take deep breaths and talk herself to calmness or utter a little prayer for it. This will give her just enough time to get in touch with her inner strengths, now buried under the stress of Toby's actions and the baby's crying. She needs a time-out from her turmoil until she regains her composure. In just a few private moments, she can "get a grip" on herself and figure out what to do next. It might be a struggle for Rachel to deal with her own feelings *first*, but it is absolutely essential in order for her to gain control.

By focusing entirely on Toby and her disruptive behavior, Rachel cannot see that her anger is coming from her own feelings of helplessness and ineffectiveness. She must get in touch with these feelings *first*. Here's how she does it. She begins by inhaling deeply, holds her breath for the count of four to get oxygen to her lungs and brain. Then she clears her emotional circuits by exhaling fully. Now it takes only a few seconds to switch her attention from Toby's behavior to what is really going on inside of her. Rachel asks herself, *What do I feel? I feel helpless,* and it doesn't feel good. Neither does her sense of failure. She has now identified and acknowledged her true feelings. It takes courage and honesty—strengths in and of themselves—to face her vulnerability at this time. She recognizes that it is *her* sense of inadequacy that disturbs her most.

By switching her focus from Toby's behavior, which she has not been able to control, to her own feelings, which she has the power to control, she feels immediately stronger. This realization helps Rachel let go of her sense of helplessness. She has a grip on her emotions; she feels her inner strengths return and her anger toward Toby subside. Her ability to cope with the outer pressure results from first reckoning with the pressure within.

Rachel is now ready to take control of the situation. First, she has to get Toby's full attention. She does not yell from across the room, as she did earlier, but walks over to where the little girl is standing, gets close to her, looks into her eyes, holds her hand, and gently touches her face. Then, using her voice of authority, she speaks firmly and seriously, punctuating her message with a hug. "Toby, I wish I could give you all of my attention right now, but first I have to talk to the repairman."

In the split second that Toby quiets down, she needs to hear words of appreciation and encouragement. This will give her the attention she wanted—only this time it is positive attention.

- "I very much appreciate your cooperation, Toby."
- "This is very helpful to me, Toby."

- "I can see how hard you are working at waiting, Toby."
- "This is very important work you are doing, Toby; waiting is not an easy thing to do, and you are doing it very well."
- "Thank you, Toby, for helping me."

Any one of these statements, together with having her mother take charge, will boost Toby's sense of security. And handling her need for attention in this way tells Toby that she matters. Rachel shows respect for her even when she is out of control—just when she needs it most.

Add to your child's repertoire of calming skills:

- a special quiet place (reserved for calming) where the child can look at books and favorite pictures
- counting
- prayers (for children to make up by themselves)

According to a guest psychologist at one of our groups, when parents don't take command of a chaotic situation, children feel as if they are on a bus speeding downhill with a driver who doesn't know how to stop it. Our being in control of such situations is vital to the child's sense of security. Gaining control amid such disorder demonstrates how calm can be achieved. Whatever method you use, whether prayer or measured breathing, give your children some responsibility for calming themselves, too.

To get an insight into testing behaviors, let's return to the analogy of your being a stranger in a strange land. Since you don't know the laws of the new land or the rules of the family you are living with, you make mistakes, large and small. At times, you go too far in finding out how far you can go. Most of the time, your host family conveys to you that you are a loved and valued member of their family. But you can't help doubt their love or your value when they yell at you in a language you don't understand

and for reasons you can't comprehend. Sometimes you test them to see if they will still love you no matter what you do. Don't we all want to know that we are loved unconditionally?

You will find it easier to cope when you accept that testing behaviors are a necessary part of a child's adaptation to his environment and not a personal attack on you.

Avoid the Quick Fix

Respect for children precludes rushing to rescue them when rescue is neither warranted nor desirable. The quick fix is a hasty attempt to assuage hurt feelings, the parent's and the child's. You can avoid impulsive fixing by taking into account your own feelings, especially in difficult situations, *before* you deal with your child's problems. This also prevents you from overreacting.

Six-year-old Charley came home from school one day and announced to his mother, "Nobody likes me." His words came as a sudden shock and surprise to Janet. She felt she had to act quickly to stop his hurt—and her own. Her tone of voice was tense as she rushed to the rescue.

"Oh, don't be ridiculous, Charley, everyone loves you—I love you, Daddy loves you, Grandpa loves you, Grandma loves you. For goodness sake, even the dog is crazy about you. You have no reason to feel that way. Here, have a chocolate-chip cookie and stop thinking such silly thoughts."

Janet intended to make Charley feel better, but something in her tone made him feel uneasy. Along with the cookie, he swallowed his need to tell her what led to his sad announcement. He had no chance now to sort out his feelings, and to make matters worse, he wondered if he really *was* ridiculous. After all, he thought, would Mom have said "don't be ridiculous" if she didn't think he already was? And what was he to make of her telling him he had no reason to feel as he did?

Let's take a look at the impact of Charley's announcement on Janet. They hit a nerve. His words dredged up sudden uncomfortable feelings that caused an unexpected outburst. Maybe at that precise moment she was preoccupied with thoughts about other troubles in her life—concerns over her marriage, the family finances, or her nagging regret over a sidelined career—and Charley's words just added to her worries. His words could have awakened long-buried feelings. Maybe he triggered a vague memory of a similar scene she had experienced in her own childhood.

Old submerged feelings, like phantoms from the past, can be ignited and hoisted to the surface in a flash. They can appear in a scowl or a grimace, or they can be heard in a tone of voice. Janet wants to rescue Charley, but her overreaction is also a signal to save herself.

Now Janet is hit by a new mix of feelings. In a fleeting moment she is struck by a wave of fears and doubts:

- *Where did I go wrong?* (self-doubt)
- *What am I supposed to do about this?* (feelings of inadequacy)
- *Maybe Charley is lonely, as I was.* (phantom from the past)
- *Good grief, he has no friends.* (catastrophizing)

An overreaction signals that something separate is going on within us. It could be one of those *divine nudges* to resolve "old business" and liberate ourselves from past hurts. We can ignore the feeling, or dismiss it, or bury it all over again. Sometimes we'll subdue it, but at other times it will continue to niggle and niggle, urging us to pay attention. It is beckoning us to take care of ourselves and heal old wounds.

- *Oh, I feel so sorry for him.* (pity)
- *Am I doing what my mother did to me?* (fear of repeating history)
- *Maybe there is something wrong with him.* (fear for the future)
- *If his father spent more time with him . . .* (displaced anger)
- *This is killing me.* (pain)

It all happens in a flash. Janet's fears and insecurities compound her pain. Any one of her concerns is enough to keep her absorbed and distracted while Charley is still waiting. Janet has to find a way to get past the initial shock and impact of his words, take hold of the turmoil within her, and regain her equilibrium. She needs time.

Buy a Little Time

Let's try the whole scene over. Charley has just said, "Nobody likes me," and this time, instead of hurrying to the quick fix, Janet deals with *her* feelings *first*. She recognizes that Charley's words have caught her off guard. She stops herself from reacting (deep breaths) and knows she has to buy a little time to recover from the shock and surprise of his words. She and Charley will have to separate.

> *Janet:* Whoa, Charley, this sounds important. Look, put your things away, go up and wash your hands and I'll have some cookies and hot chocolate waiting for you. Let's meet back in the kitchen when you are finished. I want to hear all about this.

Alone, Janet wonders, as many of us do, whether she's doing a good job as a parent. We take it for granted and feel pretty confident when our children are happy and getting along well with their peers. But when they throw us a curve, as Charley did, doubts bubble up to the surface.

Janet takes a minute for a reality check. Panic aside, she realizes that Charley is usually a happy little fellow and that he has lots of friends. Now, as *she tunes into herself*, she realizes that his words triggered a painful memory. *I would hate to for him to be as insecure as I was when I was a child.* Janet recalls how she felt when her mother brushed her off every time she tried to talk to her about her feelings. She senses she is on the brink of a deeply personal *unresolved* matter. Because this is not the time to deal with it, she separates out Charley's issue and promises herself she will take a closer look at her own uneasiness when she can give it her full attention.

Her issue set aside, now, and only now, is she able *to make room for Charley.* Janet is free to tune in to him and listen, not only with her undivided attention but with her heart as well. Five minutes are up. Charley and Janet are seated at the kitchen table and she says: "Okay, Charley, I'm listening."

This was all Janet needed to say to get him started. Charley needs no further encouragement to talk because he brings to the table his past experiences with his attentive, patient, supportive, open-minded / open-hearted, compassionate mother. He trusts that she will not judge him, criticize, condemn, or correct him. For her part, Janet knows from past experience that she can trust Charley to be honest with her and with himself. What a relief for her and for Charley to engage in such dialogue! How satisfying it is for her to be completely there for him rather than feeling she must rush to rescue him.

Charley had something on his mind. He needed a patient listener—someone who would open the way for him to sort out his thoughts and feelings. Janet did not ask, "What happened?" or "Why do you feel that way?" *Had she asked any questions at all, she would have steered him off his own course and he would have felt he had to answer her questions instead of exploring his own.* The pressure to give her specific answers—answers he might neither have nor want to reveal at that moment could discourage him from continuing the conversation.

Had Janet pressed him for answers, he might have said, as we so often hear children say, "Aw, forget it," or "Never mind," and cut off any further talk. If we crowd their internal space with our questions, they cannot take hold of their issues. They need to be free to go in their own direction without interference. Let's see how the rest of the dialogue went.

The Patient Listener

Janet: I'm listening, Charley.

Charley: Well, I know *you* like me, 'cause you're my mother. But I don't know if any one else does. Do you ever wonder if people like you?

Janet: Sometimes I do. (This tells Charley he's not the only one who feels this way.)

Charley: 'Specially when you do bad things?

Janet: What do you mean by bad, Charley?

Charley: Like not helping a friend.

Janet: Do you want to tell me more about that? (no judgments).

Charley: Well, I didn't help somebody today.

Janet: I see (no preachments, no probing).

Charley: Do you have to help people even when you don't feel like it?

Janet: Well, Charley, what would *you* say to that?

Charley: Sometimes I feel like helping and sometimes I don't.

Janet: People do feel that way (another reassurance).

Charley: Do you think I am a bad person if I don't help?

Janet: I never think you are a bad person, Charley.

Charley: Well, I didn't help my friend today and I feel bad about it.

Janet: Charley, figuring out what to do in these kinds of situations is part of growing up. What do you think about helping when you are not in a helping mood?

Charley: I think I should help anyway.
Janet: Even though you might not feel like it?
Charley: Yeah.
Janet: That's pretty grown-up thinking, Charley.
Charley: Yeah. Thanks, Mom.

Janet sensed the seriousness of Charley's problem, but she didn't jump in to tell him what she thought he ought to know. She didn't make any attempt to make him feel better by smoothing things over. She did not try to change his feelings *(you have no reason to feel that way)* or deny them *(of course everyone loves you)* or trivialize them *(don't be ridiculous)*. She sat quietly by as Charley grappled with a weighty matter. She didn't preach or try to persuade him to "do the right thing."

Janet's calm and sensitive approach to Charley's pressing matter is based on her faith in the strength of her family's values and the acceptable behaviors that they demonstrate. She trusts Charley to learn what matters from his experiences in his everyday life. From doing chores around the house he has learned to share responsibilities, from setting aside a portion of his allowance for birthday gifts for family and friends he learns the value of personal sacrifice. And from watching his parents' acts of charity, he learns how to express a generous spirit. Janet trusts that Charley has taken to heart those examples to guide him toward making good decisions. At the end of their talk, he shows that he has indeed absorbed the good values that surround him. The dialogue reflects their mutually respectful relationship.

How good it feels to be taken seriously. How good to be free from the intrusion of someone else's feelings or opinions or lessons or advice when we are struggling to find our own answers. The time Janet took to listen, with undivided attention, conveyed to Charley that he is important and worthwhile, that he is worth-her-while. If anything will boost a child's self-esteem, paying this kind of attention will.

Several mothers in a group said they didn't feel they were doing enough by "just listening." Never underestimate its power. There is far more to listening than "just listening." There's meeting the child where he is when he needs you most. Janet's attentiveness demonstrated her support and her faith in her son's ability to find his own answers. This kind of trust in our children gives them exactly what they need to trust themselves and others.

Janet respected her son's right to privacy, mindful that he could have been wrestling with something too painful or embarrassing to expose. Instead, she gave him the freedom to say whatever came to mind, to think his problem through without having to reveal more than comfort would allow. She gave him the space to come to his own conclusion by standing by him with patience and compassion.

Nineteenth-century poet Dinah Maria Mulock Craik described how it feels to have a patient listener:

> O, the comfort,
> the inexpressible comfort
> of feeling safe with a person,
> having neither to weigh thoughts
> nor measure words
> but pouring them all right out
> just as they are
> chaff and grain together,
> certain that a faithful hand
> will take and sift them,
> keep what is worth keeping
> and then with the breath of kindness
> blow the rest away.

Probing versus Respect

Some parents argued that a laid-back approach like Janet's might not result in a child confessing the error of his ways. They felt there was probably more to the story and that she should have questioned him until she found out everything that happened. From the dialogue, however, you can see that the details of the story unfolded naturally and at the same time gave Charley the chance to sort out his thoughts and feelings. Probing could have put Charley on the spot, making it hard for him to continue. He might not have been ready to give his mother the particulars of his experience. Think about the times you began to share an intimate story with a friend. Did you cautiously give one point at a time, holding back those details you were not ready to reveal? What would you have felt if your friend persisted in questioning you and pressed you for answers? It takes patience and restraint and faith in our children for them to reveal their secrets.

If we can't probe, what do we do about secrets? This bears repeating. In a world where bad things happen, at the first sign that your child seems troubled or you suspect he is bearing a secret, you will have to ask questions. Here is a nonthreatening way to open such a dialogue. *I have a feeling something is troubling you.* If you have been a patient, noncritical listener all along, this may be all the encouragement the child needs to tell you what is bothering him. However, if he does not speak up or if the burden has become too great for him to carry, he will show it in a variety of behaviors. Bed-wetting, lack of appetite, fear of going to bed, fear of the dark, fear of strangers, sleeplessness, depression, and other apparent changes will signal that he needs help. If any of these symptoms appears, or if your child's behavior is uncharacteristic of him, it is imperative to get professional help as soon as possible so that he can unburden himself.

Janet's Feelings

In a private moment, Janet is ready to take a look at what lurked beneath the surface of her overreaction. Vague as her feeling was, she sensed that there was something important in it. She thinks back to when Charley first announced that nobody likes him. She feels there is a connection between Charley's words and some old feelings from her own childhood. She recalls that whenever she wanted to talk about her feelings, her mother stifled her by dismissing her concerns and gave her cookies instead. To her great surprise, Janet sees that she repeated a behavior she desperately wanted to avoid. She even used the same dismissive words her mother had used, "Don't be ridiculous!" She has a hunch that this incident with Charley touched on other unresolved feelings between her mother and herself. Many situations with our children can be catalysts for resolving "old business."

Squabbles over messy rooms, doing chores, and thousands of other scenarios of our childhood happen again. This time our children stand in the place where we once stood and we stand in our parents' place. An incident in the present that has a strong emotional impact or stirs up uneasy feelings tells us it's time to work on "old business" and make some good come of our own history.

While we can't change the past, we *can* get a second chance to rid ourselves of unhealthy feelings that have lain dormant for years. We can give meaning to our experiences that we could not find in childhood; we can look for openings for forgiveness—for ourselves and others. In this way, without their knowing it, our children can be instrumental in helping us grow and outgrow old hurts and resentments.

If Janet's uneasiness continued long after the incident was over, if it was too vague for her to pinpoint, and if she had no relief from it, she could use a patient listener of her own to help her sort it out. If this does not help her get to the meaning or the origin of her feeling, she would be wise to engage a mental health professional who is trained to do just that.

SECRET 18

~~

Enable the Children, Empower the Children

Enable children to develop their own coping skills. Empower them to use them. The quick fix, or the rush to make things better, blocks them from taking responsibility for solving their problems on their own. When I polled parents about what they wanted most for their children, the majority said they wanted their children to be happy. Happy is good, but whose job is it? There is a world of difference between wanting our children to be happy and taking responsibility for *making* them happy. If we take upon ourselves the task of making them happy, we'll have to solve their every problem and remove every pain and worry. Even if this were possible, such overprotection would not only short-circuit their genuine feelings, but we'd interfere with their ability to build their inner strengths.

Handling Painful Situations

Take, for example, what parents are tempted to do when a child loses a beloved pet. They want to purchase a cute new puppy or kitten right away to make the child happy again, but doing so would be at the expense of intercepting the child's grief. She would lose her chance to discover the depth and meaning of her feelings. She'd miss the necessary experience of grieving, of discovering how to develop the courage to deal with loss and how to start

135

the process of healing. Lost, too, would be her opportunity to uncover a new and vital piece of information about herself—the realization that she *can* endure and survive painful situations and that there will still be a good life despite sadness and loss. Children have so much to reap from their painful experiences, not the least of which is learning to have compassion for the suffering of others. We can certainly offer comfort, but along with it, we have to give them the skills that will prepare them for whatever life hands them.

Here's what we can do when children suffer a loss. We can support them by standing by with compassion and *faith in their ability to handle their difficult experiences and pain.* As patient listeners, we can help them come to grips with the agony of loss, whether it be loss of a favorite pet, a grandparent, a friend, even the loss of a house, a school, and a community they must leave when the family relocates. Each time their hearts get broken, we can help them recognize their capacity for courage and forgiveness. When they prevail over trouble, we can make words like *courage, perseverance, resiliency, triumph,* and *success* come alive. When they win, they need to learn how to do it with grace; when they lose, lose with grace.

I knew two teenagers who contemplated suicide when they were in difficult situations. They could not see beyond their troubled moment. Neither could they see suicide as a drastic and permanent solution to a temporary problem. These boys could find no meaning in what was happening to them. We talked at length, and eventually both boys understood that they had to find enough meaning in their situations, and in their lives, to help them go on. They began by dealing with the problems they were trying to escape. Helping children find their own meaning in their experiences is a task for every parent. Each time they come to understand their painful experiences and their feelings about them, they will add to their repertoire of meanings. What a way to grow!

Children can learn important lessons for their lives from their hurtful experiences. I was not so fortunate when I was about fourteen years old. I had written a poem about a tree that I felt symbolized my life; I showed it to my best friend, and she gave it to her father to read. Nervously, I stood by as he read it. He studied it for a moment, then asked me if I had really written it. I felt insulted, though I wasn't sure why. Then he questioned me about each line, which I took as an insinuation that there was something wrong with it. I didn't know how to respond. He never said he liked it—he just dissected it and handed it back to me. Stunned and embarrassed, I went outdoors with my assumptions, tore my poem into tiny pieces, and tossed the shreds into the air. As the wind carried them away, so went my self-confidence. I mourned the loss for a long time because, try as I might, I was never able to recreate the poem.

I had no idea how to deal with what I perceived as an attack on my poem—and on me. I did not have anyone to tell me how to handle criticism, how to respond to the critic, or how to deal with my feeling of humiliation.

Critical questions:

- What can you teach your children about criticism that can help them understand it and cope with it in the present and in the future?
- How would you help them figure out how to determine if a criticism is valid and helpful?
- How would you help them to accept constructive criticism?
- How would you help them to maintain self-confidence when faced with criticism?

The Preemptive Fix

Another kind of "fix" is preemptive. Ten-year-old Alexis wanted to run for class president. She brought up the idea to her mother, Frances.

Alexis: I want to run for class president.

Frances: But you have no experience.

Alexis: Well, other people are running who don't have experience either.

Frances: What will you have to do to run?

Alexis: I'll have to make posters and a speech and have a . . .

Frances: Make posters? A speech? You're too shy to make a speech.

Alexis: I think I can do it.

Frances: If it takes you away from your schoolwork, I say no. Anyway, I don't know if you can handle the extra activities.

Alexis: I think I can. Other kids do.

Frances: Who else is thinking of running?

Alexis: Leslie.

Frances: But she's a very popular girl. She'll have lots of support, not to mention votes.

Alexis: I know.

Frances: Well, I say you have more important things to do.

When Frances recounted this conversation in a parent group, the other mothers wanted to know why she had discouraged Alexis from trying something new. She said, "I couldn't stand it if she lost, and I wanted to spare her the pain of losing." This is a clear example of excessive sentimentality.

Alexis knew she could lose the election and she was willing to risk it. Aside from her need to protect herself from pain if Alexis lost, Frances felt she was doing the right thing in sparing her child unnecessary misery. But what Alexis needed was her mother's faith in her ability to handle herself no matter what the outcome. Had Alexis gone forward with her campaign, she would have gained valuable experience and knowledge about her talents, abilities, courage, and limitations. Frances could have used a little courage herself to help her stand by Alexis, win or lose.

Think about:

- How would you have handled Alexis's desire to run for office?
- How would you handle your child's request to engage in an activity you object to?

A Last Word about Happiness

Let's take a cue from the Constitution of the United States, which does not guarantee its citizens happiness, just the freedom to pursue it. (What would our government have to do if it took responsibility for making each one of us happy?) We, too, can give our children the freedom to pursue happiness. We can give them a safe place to live, where joy happens, where they are loved, nurtured, accepted, and respected, where their goodness is cultivated, and where we bring out the best in them. Then we can leave the rest up to them.

SECRET 19

Be Yourself

Children learn how to be human beings by observing the human beings they live with. They need to see us as we are—flaws and strengths both—to know that it's okay to be one's natural self. In fairness to ourselves, we ought to consider our own personalities as precious as our children's—each a gift unto the other.

Two little girls couldn't stop giggling as one of them mimicked their teacher's manner of speaking—especially in her high-pitched tone of voice. They pretended she was speaking to her husband. "Now, Martin, sit up nice and tall, take your elbows off the table, and put the napkin in your lap. You wouldn't want me to call your mother and tell her that you have bad manners, would you?"

The girls had no image of their teacher as a person, but only as Teacher with a capital T, no matter what she was doing or where she happened to be. Like the Teacher, some of us disappear behind the persona of Parent. But we need not sacrifice our personalities when we become parents.

With all our dedication to our role as parents, we need to remind ourselves that parenting is an action—a doing—not a state of being. In our eagerness to do our job well, we tend to pay more attention to what we do than to who we are. So we read books, listen to the experts, and keep improving our parenting skills. But we have to guard against letting our personalities get lost behind a wall of stilted language and techniques. We must each speak in our own voice. Children will learn to value themselves for who they are when they observe how we value ourselves for who we are. Enjoying who we are conveys to children the joy of being oneself.

All Right, So We're Inconsistent!

Over and over, child experts tell us to be consistent with our children so that they will understand what we expect of them. What will happen, then, if you are not a consistent kind of person? Many factors affect us from day to day. How much sleep we get, how much work we have to do or have done, the foods we eat, the weather, how well we are getting along with our spouses or bosses—all influence our actions and attitudes. Stress makes us less patient than we are on relaxed days, when we tend to give our children more leeway. But stress notwithstanding, some of us have always been inconsistent, regardless of mood or circumstance. So here's a thought for those who will never win a blue ribbon for consistency. *Regardless of how you feel on a given day, the rules have to stay the same from day to day.*

On good days you may have more humor or patience in getting the rules across, and on down days, when you have less patience or fortitude, you may have to take a strictly business approach. If you cannot manage to overcome your inconsistency, take heart. There is a positive side effect: Once you have accepted your own inconsistency, you will find it is easier to accept it in your child.

Stay-at-Home Mothers

All the stay-at-home mothers in our groups were unequivocally committed to being good parents. Yet, some admitted they had some resentment at having to sacrifice their own needs for their children's sake. They eventually came to see that there was nothing wrong with their desire to fulfill themselves outside the role of mother. To that end, those who could not go to work pursued gratifying creative hobbies or meaningful volunteer work. At the same time, many mothers felt guilty for not finding enough satisfaction in "just being mothers."

When Betty Friedan's *Feminine Mystique* hit the book stores in 1963 and persuaded many stay-at-home mothers that they ought to do more than be "just mothers," some women decided to make drastic and sudden changes in their lifestyle. They wanted the freedom to choose to either stay at home or go out into the world to earn money or return to school and prepare for a career. But the choices of staying at home or working outside the home were fraught with uncomfortable feelings. At-home moms worried that motherhood was not fulfilling enough and that they were missing something important if they did not go to work or school, and mothers who chose to pursue work or school felt guilty for leaving their children. In either case, their feelings did not fit their own image of a "good" parent.

At-home mothers struggled with negative feelings and tried hard to keep them in check. They woke to feed their babies two and three times a night, fought fatigue and irritability the next day, and struggled to be cheerful and available minute to minute. Keeping a lid on their negative feelings sapped their energy. It blocked them from enjoying their relationships with their babies and their husbands. They wanted to keep up with their children's demands, even when the demands seemed unfair, unreasonable, or excessive. "But a good mother should not feel this way," one woman argued. She thought that children should have happy, cheerful mothers all the time, and so, fearing that her negative emotions would affect her children, she never expressed them. She was relieved to know that other mothers shared her feelings and fears.

Both mothers who worked at outside jobs and those who stayed at home seemed to be exerting a great effort to keep their feelings bottled up. They felt depleted, physically and emotionally. When I referred to their feelings as *negative energy,* the term hit them like a bombshell. They knew that much of their energy was going into their effort to keep their pent-up feelings in check. When they couldn't contain their feelings any longer, like steam in a pressure cooker, they boiled over. Unfortunately, the people closest to them provided an outlet.

They admitted that yelling at their husbands or children did not make them feel better. In fact, it made them feel terrible. Besides, after the momentary release, the pressure built up again. Before long, with the support and understanding of the group, they were ready to deal more honestly with their feelings.

The first step was to face their negative feelings. Though it did not fit their picture of the ideal mother, they came to understand that they were reacting naturally to the physical and emotional demands being made upon them and that it was not motherhood that was getting them down, but the strain of the job. They needed to find ways to alleviate some of their internal and external pressures. They arranged their schedules to include time for themselves; many bartered time with other mothers. They took care of each other's children to give themselves the chance to regain their sense of self. They used the time to pursue an education, to develop crafting skills, or even have an occasional day at a spa. These barter arrangements helped each one establish balance in her life, making it possible to enjoy both the time she spent as a mother and the creative or restful time she took for herself.

What You Need to Know about Mistakes

Many mothers worry that the mistakes they make in how they handle their children will do irreparable damage. We are not talking here about anything that could qualify as child abuse; we're talking about innocent acts that had good intentions. Yet, some parents suffer debilitating regret and guilt over their mistakes, no matter how small. The scenarios throughout the book have shown how parents can be totally unaware that their well-intentioned actions could turn out to be mistakes.

Let's take a look at mistakes from a fresh angle. A good tip comes from the word itself. A mis-*take* is an action we take *in good faith*, expecting a desired outcome, but one that does not turn out the way we hope. We act in the belief that we are teaching or protecting our children and showing them that we care about them. At other times, we might act before we have thought a situation through. Though we might regret the *way* we reacted, we're still of the mind that we were being as good a parent as we knew how to be. Therefore, we have absolutely no reason to question our actions. So, our *take* on the action is that we are doing the right thing. An unwanted result means that we had a wrong take on the action—a miss-take.

In his very informative book *Back to the Family,* author Ray Guarendi surveyed one hundred parents to find out what it took for them to raise happy, high-achieving, and well-adjusted children. Every person interviewed for the survey, regardless of his or her background or personal experience, had a strong commitment to the family. Some mothers and fathers were fortunate enough to have been well-parented themselves. They in turn grew up to be naturally good parents. It was in their bones. Others, not so lucky, had to leach out of their bones the *miss-takes* their parents had made. Once done, they were free to be the kind of parents they wanted to be and could become. Whether their individual abilities were natural or learned, when asked if they ever made mistakes, they all answered with both humility and candor, "Every day."

What distinguished these mothers and fathers from less successful parents was their willingness to be honest with themselves and to be flexible. Instead of blaming their children when they failed to get results, they reevaluated their parenting methods to see how they could change what they were doing. They had no trouble admitting that parenting was on-the-job training. Had they started out thinking of themselves as "experts," they would have confined themselves to a narrow way of thinking and acting. You become the expert when your child's personality is no longer a mystery to you.

The parents in the survey were willing to examine their actions, toss out what did not work, and try new methods and ideas. They did not feel they had to be right all the time. Neither did they have the kind of defenses that would prevent them from admitting their limitations. They knew they would make mistakes, but having made them, they acknowledged them and committed themselves to not repeating them. It's easy to see why their children were able to work toward their full potential and have a good time doing it. That is precisely what their parents were doing. It was clear to Dr. Guarendi that successful parents are not exempt from making mistakes but that they learn from the many mistakes they make.

By paying attention to the results of your actions, you can tell if you are doing the right thing or if you have made a mistake. Now, what is a good way to handle actions or words you regret? How about saying something like this: "I feel I made a mistake last week and I've had time to rethink what I said about [chores, or homework, or friends, etc.] and I'd like to suggest something else." If you feel that your child was hurt by a decision you made, he would appreciate an apology. It sets a good example and it opens up a chance for forgiveness. Isn't this the way we want our children to handle their mistakes?

Dr. Guarendi said:

"Excellence in child-rearing does not evolve from making fewer mistakes than everybody else. It evolves from making plenty of mistakes and learning from them."

SECRET 21

We Live in the Past, Present, and Future All at Once

In a previous chapter, you saw how past experiences affected Charley's mother in the present and influenced how she reacted to him. Fears for the future will likewise influence the way we respond to our children in the present. For example, what parent hasn't worried that her child's misdemeanors, like lying, will turn into a permanent character trait or, worse still, lead to a life-long career of crime? When that happens, we don't handle the child's present action in the context of the moment but project into the future, and with a sense of urgency, we decide that we must end the bad behavior before it is too late. This is not to say that the undesirable acts in the present should be ignored. It is to say that we need not panic.

Phantoms of the past sneak into the present and affect our reactions, the future spawns worries that can dictate our reactions in the present, and both sabotage the present by robbing us of objectivity. Charley's mother suddenly became aware of long-dormant memories and recognized their effect on the present. Rather than ignore the signal, she dealt with it by confronting the old issue and resolving it.

An antidote to worrying about the future is to stay focused on the present. This does not mean we should be unconcerned for the future. Of course, we need to be mindful that today's parenting will have a profound effect on tomorrow's child. But let it be *positive* concern. Instead of worrying about the worst that could happen, focus on a proactive approach of building positive strengths and skills for the future. If we bear in mind that childacts—lying, for example—are not prophesies of doom, we'll handle them without fear.

How to Handle Children's Lying

Lying is one of the behaviors parents feel they must nip in the bud as early as possible before it becomes a habit. Usually, children's lies are childacts meant to preserve their good boy / good girl image in their parents' eyes or to avoid punishment. Or it's a spur-of-the-moment attempt to save face. To make sure our children are not lying, we sometimes resort to testing their honesty. For example, how often do we ask a question to which we already have the answer? Or we ask a question in such a confrontational manner that the child tries to save face by lying. I did that once and regretted it the minute it spilled from my lips. Here's what happened.

My three-year-old daughter, Andrea, and I were the only ones at home. I was in the kitchen and Andrea was upstairs taking a nap. That is, I thought she was taking a nap until the odor of peppermint came wafting through the house.

I raced up the stairs, calling out, "Are you playing with the toothpaste?" (Who else, if we were the only ones at home?) Thinking I was angry, Andrea answered defensively, "No!" As I reached the bathroom, there she stood, her long hair covered in green toothpaste, which matched the walls, the floor, and the toilet.

Did I ask Andrea if she was playing with the toothpaste to test her honesty, or did I just blurt out the question without thinking? Was Andrea trying to save face or did she, too, just answer without thinking? Whatever the reason, that kind of mindless question turns out to be a test of the child's honesty. It would have been more forthright to wait and see for myself what Andrea was doing. Then, upon seeing the little green apparition and the mess she'd made, I could have merely said, "Let's clean up." Or, having blurted out the question, when I saw her, I could have answered it for myself: "Yes, I see you are playing with the toothpaste." In this honest manner, I would have given my child no reason to lie.

Colleen had a similar experience. Just as she was entering the living-room, she saw her ten-year-old son, Barry, throw a ball at the ceiling. It came crashing down on a lamp.
"Are you playing ball in the living-room?" she screamed.
That led Barry to think she had not seen him throw the ball, so he screamed back, "No."

Barry lied to escape responsibility. He knew he had made a mistake, but he did not want his mother to disapprove of him or think less of him. And he didn't want to be punished. So we can handle these situations without placing our children in a position to lie. Instead of asking the superfluous question, make a statement. All Barry's mother had to do, and all I had to do, was to state the obvious: "Let's clean up the mess and talk about the consequences later." And speaking of consequences, I highly recommend *Unconditional Parenting,* by Alfie Kohn, who strongly advocates that children take an active role in deciding what *they* should do about their unacceptable actions. By dictating consequences

---

Your child's honesty in these kinds of situations depends on the way you handled them in the past.

- Take a look at your reactions and see if they encouraged your child to feel free to be honest.
- Does your child know that he or she can talk openly with you without fear of punishment or criticism?

---

or punishments, parents rob children of the valuable experience of taking responsibility for their actions and correcting them.

Some mothers said they assure their children they won't be punished if they tell the truth. They will, however, be punished if they lie. The child who trusts his parents to listen, and who does not fear punishment, will more than likely be honest with them. And the parent who trusts his or her child need not make such bargains.

The following vignette asks for your understanding. Set aside any emotional reaction, stay focused on the present, and leave out fears for this little girl's future. Let's practice some objectivity here.

Adelaide came into the veterinarian's office with her younger sister, Emma, her father, and their little dog, Tiger. When the vet summoned them to go into the examining room, both girls stood up. In a voice loud enough for everyone in the waiting room to hear, Emma announced, "You're not going in with Tiger and *I* am. Daddy said so."

The door closed behind them and Adelaide slumped in her seat. Crushed, she glanced around, fearing that everyone in the waiting room was aware of her humiliation. Shortly thereafter, a young woman came in with her little dog and sat down next to Adelaide.

"Is your dog sick?"

"No," the woman replied, "we're just here for a shot."

Adelaide's face brightened. She pushed herself upright, pulled her shoulders back, and, managing to look both forlorn and heroic, she said, "My dog is too, but I love him so much I just couldn't stand to see him get a shot, so I'm waiting out here until it's all over."

Yes, Adelaide lied, but she also desperately needed to feel better about herself. Her lie helped her get through the pain of being excluded and embarrassed. Is she destined always to make excuses for herself? Is she on her way to a life of crime? If she has been honest all along, this incident will not change her into a criminal. An occasional incident of lying does not define the child's total character or make a habitual liar of her.

Telling tales and lying are not the same. When it comes to children telling their wonderfully imaginative tales, who would want to stop them? Do we fear (Futurethink) they will never be able to distinguish between fantasy and reality? Here's a way to respond without discouraging a young child's creativity: "I love the stories you tell. I hope that someday you will write them down and make a book of them."

Let the children dream their dreams and pretend. Don't we, in fact, even encourage them to indulge in fantasy at certain times—like when we tell them Santa brought their gifts and the Tooth Fairy left coins under their pillows? We won't make children honest by forcing them to swap their little fantasies for reality.

Trust that your child will pick up the value of honesty from the honest people that surround him. If you are still worried that your imaginative child will grow up not knowing fantasy from reality, try to remember that all the advancements of humankind were the work of dreamers.

Myopic Parenting

Shortsightedness is another miss-take. It happens when parents do not stop to consider the long-range effects of their parenting methods. For example, Fred Jones thought he was doing the right thing by repeatedly refusing his son Pat's requests for toys. Fred believed that giving his son negative experiences early in life would train the boy to handle disappointment throughout life. But Fred ignored warnings of possible other outcomes. Instead of learning how to handle disappointment—the lesson Fred wanted to teach—Pat was showing signs of feeling he deserved nothing. He might turn that around later and grow up wanting everything. Such negative "training" could impair his ability to trust anyone, or he might trust everyone indiscriminately.

Fred's approach led to a group discussion on the effects of

How you say no, saying no arbitrarily, or saying no too often, affects children in different ways. Ask yourself:

- Will your saying no make them want everything, or will it make them feel they are not deserving of anything?
- If we humiliate children, will they become accustomed to feeling humiliated and continue to create situations for themselves and others that always end in humiliation?
- Will they need humiliation in their lives because it is familiar and they learned to endure it?
- Will they continue to be humiliated, or will they become the ones who humiliate others or themselves?
- If they grow up with feelings of rejection, will rejection become a way of life for them?
- Will they continue with behaviors that constantly result in their being rejected, or will they become the rejecters?

tough parenting methods on a child's character. Here are the important points the parents made that all parents need to consider: A better way to fortify our children for the future is to make sure they feel secure and safe; that's what it takes to handle adversity. We need to make every effort to avoid disappointing them or saying no too often. This does not mean that we must give in to every request children make; with so many new gadgets and toys and snack foods to attract them in the stores, we have to draw the line somewhere. But it's how we turn them down that matters.

Fred would have benefited greatly from the advice found in Adele Faber and Elaine Mazlish's *How to Talk So Kids Will Listen and Listen So Kids Will Talk*. In this book, a mother in one of their groups takes a pencil and paper and writes down the second item her son requested in a gift shop. Taking notice and making a wish list satisfied the boy enough to end his pleadings. He didn't get the object, and the parent didn't yield to pressure, but the refusal happened in a loving, thoughtful, nonhumiliating way. If the requested item is financially out of reach, the same benign approach avoids embarrassing the child. *If you really want it, we can work something out. If you're willing to earn money doing extra chores, you will be able to save up for half the cost and Dad and I will pay the other half.* This technique is not just a matter of manners; it acquaints children with the ways of consideration and kindness.

With this sort of background, we hope our children will settle for nothing less than these qualities in the relationships they form throughout their lives. Children will draw upon their repertoire of good experiences to shape their character. This happens when we practice positive Futurethink.

How Humor Helps

Life without humor is deadening to the spirit. Humor helps us accept our imperfections. Traditional Jewish humor, African American humor, and Irish humor are all excellent examples of this power. Some of the humor in the literature of beleaguered people holds up a mirror to them and reflects back their foibles, frailties, and follies.

In the worst of times, it sustains them individually and collectively. It enables them to endure the intolerable conditions of their lives and bad luck. Humor is a buoy that keeps people afloat in a sea of misery. It is a lifeline.

Laughter is a magical outlet that transforms deep-seated pain into fortitude. It heals the heart and bonds us one to another. It helps us maintain a healthy outlook and a way to accept our own limitations. Humor is a gift for a lifetime. We saw it work wonders in our groups. It often softened the sting of recognizing, admitting, and accepting our mistakes. The words *humor, human,* and *humility* come from the same root, reminding us not to take ourselves too seriously.

Humor played a large role in our developing humility in our groups. It helped us accept our humanness and fallibility when-

155

ever our individual efforts or collective wisdom backfired. Here's a true story that had us laughing our heads off at ourselves.

Lily came to a meeting wanting to know how to handle five-year-old Jason's new habit of kicking the walls when he got angry. At the end of a lengthy discussion, she left the meeting with enough ideas, self-confidence, and determination "to stay calm no matter what."

The following week she reported on her progress. After another wall-kicking incident, instead of flying off the handle as she had done before, she sent Jason to his room so that they could both calm down. A few minutes later Lily entered his room, cool, collected, and excited over the prospect of using her new and improved parenting skills. She started by validating his feelings.

"I see that you are very angry," she said calmly and proudly.

Jason was so completely taken aback by his mother-turned-stranger that he got up and stormed out of the room, yelling over his shoulder, "I *hate* it when you talk to me like that!"

We need to realize that our children might not be ready for any sudden change in us. It may take time for them to understand and accept the differences in the way we respond to them.

~

Learn How to Handle Your Differences

Linguist Deborah Tannen's superenlightening and delightful book *You Just Don't Understand* describes some of the ways men and women differ in their use of language and how it affects their respective needs. The title of John Gray's book, *Men Are from Mars, Women Are from Venus*, sums up the extent of the differences between men and women, while the Broadway musical *My Fair Lady* offers a simple solution to the trouble between the sexes. Without a trace of self-consciousness, Professor Henry Higgins sings, "Why can't a woman be like a man?"

How many of us expect our spouses to be just like us? Even when partners express their differences openly to each other, especially in knotty situations, they may not communicate or hear each other's underlying meanings. Having different backgrounds, and different priorities, strongly influences the way mothers and fathers approach situations involving their children.

Ten-year-old Bobby was sitting at the kitchen table doing his homework while his mother, Jan, prepared dinner. They heard the back door slam as Bobby's father stormed into the house.

Jan (mutters loud enough for Bobby to hear her): There he goes again. What awful crime do you think we committed this time?

Mark (coming into the kitchen): Bobby! Get out there and put your bike in the garage, *Now!*

Jan: Calm down, Mark. He'll do it when he's through with his homework.

Mark: I said *Now.*

Jan: He just has one more math problem to do.

Mark: What he *has* is a bike in the driveway blocking me from getting my car into the garage, and what he *has* is a new bike rusting in the rain, and what he has to *do* is to get up and get out there to put his bike away or he won't have a bike to put away.

Jan: I'll put it away. Let him finish his homework.

Mark: No, *he'll* put it away, and he'll do it now, and I'd appreciate your staying out of this.

Jan: You are being totally unreasonable, Mark. You'd better put your bike away, Bobby, since your father is in one of his moods.

This kind of confrontation happens every day in homes across America. Mark's and Jan's backgrounds shaped their different priorities (one not better or worse than the other, just different). Jan's top priority for Bobby is his education. To Mark, obeying rules and taking personal responsibility comes first. Jan does not handle anger well. Mark thinks it's healthy to express anger openly. Both have Bobby's interest at heart and both are dedicated to being good parents.

Mark signaled his state of mind when he slammed the door and stormed into the house. Fearing an attack on Bobby was imminent, Jan immediately snapped into her mother-hen role and proceeded to protect her son, not realizing she was doing so at Mark's expense. Her spontaneous reaction allowed no time to consider how her protectiveness could impact on Bobby's relationship with his father. She did not realize her intervention could have heightened Bobby's fears if it made him wonder, *What would my father do to me if my mother didn't stop him?* And how does Bobby perceive his father's anger? If Jan did not trust Mark to have a valid reason for his anger, how could Bobby? Jan's "take" on the situation was that Bobby needed to be rescued from his father's wrath. And her take on the situation was that she had to protect her son. It turned out to be a miss-take when her good intention had the potential to damage the relationship between Bobby and his father, as well as her own relationship to her husband.

Jan not only ignored the intensity of Mark's anger but also added to it when she asked him to calm down. He took her rebuke as an attempt to control him, or worse, to belittle him in front of his son. Coming home from work after a stressful day, he couldn't get his car into the garage, a new bicycle was getting wet, and so was he. It rankled Mark that Bobby was irresponsible and lacking the values he thought he had taught him. Worried for Bobby's future, Mark wanted to emphasize that obedience and responsibility are qualities that Bobby must develop in order to succeed in life.

Jan is equally concerned about her son's future. Because she considers education to be the stepping-stone to his success in life, she is angry with Mark for interrupting Bobby's homework. It upsets her that Mark does not share her values. She does not consider their views to be equally valid; to her, they are mutually exclusive. Concerned about the effect of Mark's anger on Bobby's psyche and his future, Jan made herself a buffer between Mark and his son.

How can father and son work out their problems together? How can Mark know his effect on his son if Jan blocks their access to each other? How will Bobby learn about trust if his parents don't appear to trust each other? Husbands want their wives' support—or as I have heard countless times from fathers in my groups, they want their wives to be on their "team." Mark felt his authority had been undermined when Jan countermanded or questioned his orders, especially in full view of their child. Mark and Jan hardly ever concede to each other. How else can Mark and Jan handle their differences in such an emotionally loaded situation? In the replay, respect changes the way they respond to both the situation and to each other.

Jan hears the door slam.

Jan: Uh, oh, sounds like Dad's upset. (Her tone is sympathetic.)

Mark: Bobby, get out there and put your bike away!

Bobby: But, Dad . . .

Mark: I don't want to hear any excuses, son—just put your bike in the garage, *now!*

Bobby: Can I just finish this last math problem?

Mark: No, Bobby, you can finish it after you put your bike away. Now go.

Mark and Jan discuss this matter after Bobby has gone to bed.

Mark: I appreciated your letting me handle the bike situation with Bobby. I know you would have preferred to have Bobby finish his homework, but every minute the new bike sat out there in the rain I saw it turning into a pile of rust.

Jan: It isn't easy getting him to take responsibility. Maybe if we let the bike turn into a pile of rust he'd learn his lesson. (Though she disagrees with his approach, she supports his priority.)

Mark: No, that's too expensive a price to pay. Besides, it wasn't just the bike, it was also a matter of his being considerate of others. At first I thought about putting it in the garage myself, but then I got mad. I thought if he had to get wet he'd know how I felt and he'd learn the lesson.

Jan: But Mark, this is what concerns me. Do you think Bobby would regard you as the inconsiderate one for interrupting his homework? And Mark, I have to tell you I am somewhat concerned about how your coming on so

strong affects Bobby. I'd hate to see him withdraw from
you out of fear or anger.

Mark: I think I better straighten all this out with Bobby.

Jan gave Mark an opportunity to evaluate himself. She felt secure enough in their relationship to be honest and open about
his behavior without being critical. This kind of nonjudgmental
give-and-take dialogue encouraged Mark to correct himself. In
this scenario, each parent respected the other's opinions and
values. They helped each other grow as persons and as parents.
They gave each other the kind of support each needs to get
through the stresses of daily living. By refraining from excessive
sentimentality, Jan did not rush to shield Bobby from his father.
She stood back and let father and son handle their problem.

Mark (sitting down next to Bobby on his bed): Bobby, you
know I was very angry when I came home tonight.

Bobby: I know, Dad, and I'm sorry I left my bike in the driveway. I really meant to put it away, but I just ran into the
house when it started to rain, and well, I just forgot.

Mark: Well, I'm sorry too, for coming in and sounding like
a bully, but can you understand that I was tired and upset
that I couldn't just drive into the garage? And you know
how I feel about you taking responsibility for yourself.

Bobby: I know, Dad, I'll try to do better.

Mark: So will I.

There's a way to deal with these issues without declaring war.
As long as there is no threat of physical or mental harm to the
child, fathers and mothers can agree not to undermine each other
and reserve their disagreements for private moments. However,
this does not mean that parents need to be in full agreement all
of the time. Parents are individuals and each has his or her own
opinions and thoughts. When they exchange opposing views,
children can benefit from seeing how their parents handle their

differences. If the argument heats up, assure your children that your relationship is strong enough to handle it. They also need to see how their parents resolve their disagreements and to see that relationships can and do survive strong differences of opinion.

Marital Discord

A word about the effects of strained marital relationships on children. In all my years in groups, I observed that the parents with satisfying and healthy relationships were more likely to have satisfying and healthy relationships with their children. Parents with troubled marriages had great difficulty concealing their heartache and turmoil from their children. When they heard their parents argue, the children tended to blame themselves for the discord. Go back to the foreign family you were placed in and picture the adults in charge quarreling and angry. Would you wonder whether it was because of you?

Professional counseling helped many couples resolve their personal issues, and as a result they became more relaxed parents. The joy of a good marriage spills over to children and the joylessness of a troubled marriage also spills over.

An unhappy marriage is like a house on fire; it makes the air dense—so dense at times, the children can hardly breathe or laugh or sing. Though Jan felt the need to protect her child, she did not stop to consider "at what cost" to the other parent. Here are questions to ask yourself before putting yourself between your child and your spouse:

- Will my protectiveness cause my child to lose respect for his other parent?
- Will I cause him to fear his other parent?
- Will I make him resent me for interfering with his relationship with his other parent?
- Will my protection condition my child always to look for

someone to rescue him instead of dealing directly with people with whom he is in conflict?

- How will my interference affect my relationship with my spouse?
- Am I making my child see me as the "good guy" and his other parent as the "bad guy?"

We need to get comfortable with the idea that we don't have to fix every situation for our children. It is sometimes hard to know when to step in, and when to step back. Staying neutral is fine as long as there is no abuse. At the first sign of physical or verbal abuse, however, protect your child.

Help Children Learn from Life's Crushing Blows

Carla brought this problem to our group. Her nine-year-old daughter, Cindy, complained that her friend Fanny did not want to be her friend any more. Carla wanted to know whether she should call Fanny's mother who, according to Fanny, doesn't like Cindy either, or should she stay out of it. Should she talk to Fanny? Should she try to make Cindy feel better? Should she ignore it? Situations like this are loaded with valuable issues that reach far into the future. This may be the first, but it certainly won't be the last time that Cindy encounters people who will not like her or who will turn against her.

Being rejected raises self-doubt. Though Cindy might not be able to articulate all of her feelings as clearly as they are stated here, these questions could be very real concerns now and in the future: *Who can I trust? Can I trust myself to pick the right people to be my friends? Am I willing to risk being hurt again? How can I know if there is something wrong with me or with the other person? Will I ever get over the hurt? What do people do when they are embarrassed or frustrated? What do I do with my anger over being treated so badly? Why are people cruel? Am I supposed to be cruel back? Should I tell Fanny how I feel?*

Look at the range of doubts and questions that stem from this single incident. They call for more than merely talking to Fanny or her mother. Cindy is pondering questions she never had to deal with before, and she has to make decisions she never had to make before. She is realizing, perhaps for the first time in her life, that having friends makes people vulnerable and having close relationships means that she'll have to be willing to take a chance on being hurt again. With Carla as her patient listener, Cindy will have the opportunity to ask these questions aloud and sort out her feelings. It's at times like these that children discover meanings and values for themselves. Ask your child to tell you all the feelings children might have after having been "kicked out" of a friendship. You might be surprised to hear the depth of their feelings and insights.

When Children Hurt

How can we avoid feeling pain when our children are suffering? If it is suffering caused by physical injury or illness, there is no doubt that we will suffer along with them. But less serious problems can cause parents pain as well. Our feelings are hard to handle when our children experience insult or rejection by their peers, when they are unfairly treated by their teachers, or when they are ignored or bullied on the playground. It helps to remember that one of the rights children have is the right to the low points of their lives. Such instances, painful as they may be, are opportunities to help them develop inner strengths and coping skills.

Children also suffer from stress. Every toddler finds it out the first time his forehead meets the corner of the kitchen table. We can't protect children from all undue stress (nor do we ever want to cause it,) but when it does happen, help them learn how to deal with it. The first step is to put words to their feelings to enable them to distinguish one feeling from another—anger, stress, sadness, etc. Now you have given them a way to know what is happening to them the next time around. Let your children know that stress can seriously affect their ability to think clearly and act sensibly. Teach your children any of the new coping skills, like breathing exercises to calm their inner turmoil.

Hundreds of former cult members I interviewed told me they were unable to deal with the stress they experienced in college. For some, it was a lifelong pattern; for others it was the momentary strain of exams, lack of finances, or broken romances. But whatever the cause, their inability to cope with the pressures of their lives made them vulnerable and especially susceptible to the enticements of cults. Other young people I met sought escape from pressure through drugs, alcohol, and, in some tragic cases, suicide. Learning to deal effectively with stress can be their safeguard against the destructive choices others make under pressure and can one day save their lives.

How Children Learn about Themselves

A child at play learns about himself—his abilities and his limitations. He tests, he tries, he succeeds, and he fails, gathering vital information as he goes through the day. He finds out what scares him, what hurts him, what makes him laugh, what makes him cry, what decisions to make, and how to make them.

John and Gloria Wright were watching their four-year-old son, Adam, climb the ladder on a playground sliding-board. Each time he got to the top he turned around and looked as if he was going to jump. Fearing for the little boy's safety, John wanted to stop him, but Gloria suggested that her husband take a second look at what Adam was doing. On closer inspection, John saw that Adam carefully considered the distance from the top of the ladder to the ground. He climbed to the top, turned around, looked down, then went down to a step he thought was high enough to handle, yet safe enough to jump from, and only then did he jump.

Now John saw a cautious little boy engaged in a studied process of judging space and distance—a little boy who did not take dangerous chances. He felt a surge of pride in his son's good judgment. Gloria certainly would have dissuaded Adam if she thought he was in danger of getting hurt. But by paying close attention, she could see something important going on besides his just jumping off a ladder.

Adam was learning about himself—about his willingness to accept a challenge, about how much courage he had, how much strength he had, how much determination, perseverance, and ability. He was learning about his limits, his judgment, his trust, and his faith in himself. In all of this, his mother *refrained from interfering*. She knew that self-discovery and many of life's lessons happen through childwork.

Self-esteem

Where does self-esteem come from? Most of the parents in my groups said they thought it came from praising their children— and the more praise, the more self-esteem. So imagine how puzzled they were when their children responded to their praise with statements like, "No, I'm not." If the parents attributed the child's remark to modesty, they did not realize that external praise needs to resonate with the child's own sense of pride in his abilities.

Words of praise have meaning when they reflect the children's own sense of accomplishment and validate their positive image of themselves. Self-esteem comes from the *inner knowledge* of one's own worth and ability. It is a matter of affirmation of who they are and what they can achieve. It refers to the worth of the whole person. And we communicate it with more than words. Children see themselves in our eyes—how we look at them tells them at least as much as, if not more than, words of praise. Looking at children with eyes that say "I know who you are and I believe in you" is what kindles their self-esteem.

Rita came to our group asking how she could build up her twelve-year-old daughter Polly's self-esteem. She said Polly "fell to pieces" when she received anything less than an "A" for her schoolwork. Rita assured us that neither she nor her husband pressured her for high grades. It appeared that Polly was putting enormous pressure on herself to succeed. Many children set high standards for themselves, but they don't fall apart when they fail to reach them. Why did Polly?

In our discussion, we learned that Polly felt insecure about herself in other ways—her looks, her weight, her perception that she did not fit in with her peers. Was she trying to compensate for all of her concerns by getting high marks? Did "A" stand for acceptance in Polly's mind? Just being twelve could be a major factor in the pressure she felt.

Puberty is a difficult time of physical change and hormone-driven mood swings. Like many adolescents, Polly needs a great deal of support and understanding as she struggles with serious issues of image, acceptance, and self-esteem. Once she gets a handle on these matters, she might not place so much importance on her grades. Luckily, neither she nor her parents have to go it alone.

Many schools across the nation have trained peer counselors who offer resources and helpful suggestions. School guidance counselors are particularly sensitive to the stresses of this age group and they can provide added support and coping skills. Youth groups in churches, synagogues, and other community organizations welcome newcomers, and they fill a very real need for the adolescent to "belong." If Polly has a special hobby or talent, joining a group would put her in touch with others who share her interest. Above all, Polly needs her parents' faith in her ability to pull through this rough period.

Some parents react to their children's high marks as if these were a sign of their own success. The good report card makes the rounds of friends and family, often to the embarrassment of the child. Besides the flurry of "whajagets" circulating around the classroom at report card time, children want their teachers and parents to appreciate the work that went into getting the good grades. They feel that focusing solely on the mark overlooks their time and effort, knowledge and skill.

If your child comes rushing in announcing she got an "A" on

her test, she would appreciate your taking the time and interest in the work that went into it. She'd love to hear, "Well, let's take a look at what earned that A." Then, by adding thoughtful comments on the merits of the work, coupled with your time, attention, and interest, you will affirm your child's self-worth. Some child experts have trouble with the statement "I'm so proud of you." They think children should strive for their own sense of achievement and pride. They suggest, instead: "I am very impressed with the work you've done and you have every reason to be proud of the fine job you did." Going easy on *your* pride makes room for the child's pride in him or herself.

A mother brought another problem to our group. She thought her son was "knocking himself out" trying to compete with his highly successful father. Sometimes the parents' success inspires the child to succeed, whereas other children may feel defeated from the start.

In any case, parents need to know how their own success affects each child. How parents handle their success also matters. High-achieving parents who do not tolerate their own mistakes unwittingly communicate to their children that to err is unforgivable.

How do we help children value and accept themselves, flaws and all? It begins with our valuing and accepting ourselves for who we are and at the same time expressing our desire to keep improving ourselves. There's a big difference between saying "I think I'll take some adult education courses" and self-deprecating remarks like "I'm so dumb." Putting ourselves down gives children the impression we do not accept ourselves as we are, and it can rub off. We don't want them to mimic such attitudes and become overly critical of themselves. It's also a good idea to set the example of improvement and growth. And, if we think about it, none of us wants our children to regard their mothers or fathers as "dumb."

If we accept our children for who they are, as they are, how do we correct them? Teaching is always necessary. When it is done in a loving and compassionate spirit, it reaches mind and heart. We can hope that the example you set before them of striving to do better will inspire them to better themselves. However, as I mentioned earlier, teaching is not the same as criticizing. Harsh criticism can impinge on a child's self-esteem and create self-doubt. Therefore, we have to know which child comes to us with a laid-back attitude toward himself and can handle constructive criticism and which child takes even the slightest criticism as a personal rebuke. A far more effective way for children to recognize their errors is to encourage them to evaluate themselves.

When I was teaching, I started each school year by setting out the academic goals, and I said I would take half the responsibility for our success or failures. At report card time, I asked each student to write a letter to tell me whether they felt we had achieved our goals and the reasons why we had or had not succeeded. Feeling free from any value judgments, every student who felt we did not achieve success blamed himself or herself and stated the reasons why! They took their self-evaluations seriously and were motivated to move forward and do better.

Self-esteem and Intuition

We are born with an inner knowing—a divine notion of what is good for us and what is not. It's a built-in radar system that senses danger, warning us to take heed. Even tiny babies can pick up on bad vibes in people and react by tensing their muscles or screaming their little hearts out. They sense whom they can or cannot trust right from the start. If we can help them hold on to that first line of defense, they will be able to sniff out danger all their lives.

Unfortunately, in our present politically correct atmosphere, we want to be "fair" or nonjudgmental, and as a result, some of us wind up ignoring our intuitive reactions. We tend to disregard the uneasiness we feel in the presence of people who could harm us. Furthermore, many of us have come to believe that all we need to get along in this highly technological society is our intellect—that if we just use the old noodle, we'll be able to tell the good guys from the bad. Well, if we do in fact use our heads, how come so many of us get taken in by the bad guys— the con artists, the abusers, the charlatans? In a world overrun with bad guys, we'd better take another look at the importance of intuition and see what we can do to strengthen it in our children—and while we're at it, see how we can fine-tune our own.

What does it takes to help children develop their natural intuition, learn to trust and rely on it? Above all, children must learn to trust their feelings—which, after all, is what intuition is all about. And trusting their feelings depends largely on how *you* handle and respect those feelings. We're usually supportive when we agree with the child's feeling, but suppose we see no reason for a feeling a child expresses. With a well-intentioned desire to have their children see things in another light, or to make them feel better, how often have you heard parents say "You shouldn't feel that way." But is this the only choice?

In the following scenario, Tim and Jean Smith are faced with a conflict: on the one hand, they want to respect their daughter's feelings; on the other, they want her to be polite, even if it means overlooking her natural feelings. Here's what happened:

Tim was eager to impress his boss with his capabilities as a newly hired executive and as a family man. Anticipating a visit from his boss's wife, Jean spent several hours the previous week rehearsing good manners with their five-year-old daughter, Betsy. Completely devoted to making a good impression, neither parent gave much thought to how Betsy might intuitively react to Mrs. Bluefeather. The fateful day arrived.

Instead of politely saying "I'm pleased to meet you," as they had practiced, Betsy bolted from the room without a word. Embarrassed, Jean apologized for Betsy's rude behavior. After Mrs. Bluefeather left, Jean headed for Betsy's room.

Now put yourself in Jean's position. What would you have said if you were Jean? Write down your feelings, then set your notes aside to look at later. Now, as you enter Betsy's room, ask yourself what upset you most about her behavior. Her bad manners? Damage to Dad's image? Your embarrassment? Betsy's reason for dashing out?

Jean's first reaction was anger. As she headed for Betsy's room, she was thinking: *How could she do this to us? What will happen now? What will Mrs. Bluefeather think of us and what will she tell her husband? What is the matter with that child? Is she spiteful? too stupid to learn good manners? mean-spirited? She ought to be punished! If I had done that my parents would have killed me.*

This is what Jean said:

Jean: Betsy, what in the world is wrong with you? Do you know how much you embarrassed your father and me and heaven knows what Mrs. Bluefeather thought! How could you be so rude after we told you how important her visit was to us? Why did you run out like that?
Betsy: I didn't like that lady.
Jean: How can you not like her? You don't even know her.
Betsy: I just got a bad feeling.
Jean: I don't know what kind of feeling you got, but I am sure it had nothing to do with her. She happens to be a very nice person.

Jean meant well. She wanted to teach Betsy not to prejudge people. She wanted her to be polite. And she wanted the boss's wife to see that she and her husband are doing a fine job as parents. However, the words Jean used nibbled away at Betsy's trust in herself. Betsy had an honest reaction to Mrs. Bluefeather, and she felt she had to get away from her. Her action had nothing to do with being reasonable. Because children assume mothers know best, Jean's defense of Mrs. Bluefeather and her criticism of Betsy's feelings made Betsy doubt herself. How can she believe in herself if she cannot trust her own feelings to be valid? Then, reacting to her mother's question, Betsy wondered, *What is wrong with me?* She could not separate herself from her feelings. *(I feel, therefore I am.)* In the end, both her trust in herself and her self-esteem were diminished.

Betsy did what came naturally; she withdrew from someone who made her feel uncomfortable. She needed her parents to give her the benefit of the doubt that she had a reason for her action. Caught up in the pressure of the moment, Jean was not able to realize that *something must have caused Betsy to act that way.* Trust would have made it possible for Jean to consider the possibility, and her trust in Betsy would generate the child's trust in herself.

Let's try it again. This time, Jean enters her daughter's bedroom with the purpose of finding out what the behavior *meant to Betsy.*

Jean: Betsy, I never saw you react to a guest like that before.
Betsy: I didn't like that lady.
Jean: Tell me about that.
Betsy: I got a bad feeling.
Jean: Did you ever have that feeling with anyone else?
Betsy: Yes, when I don't like a person.
Jean: Tell me more about the feeling.
Betsy: It just makes my tummy feel bad.
Jean: This is a very important feeling for you to have.
Betsy: Are you mad at me for running out?
Jean: No, I'm not mad. I can see why you felt you had to leave. But the next time you feel that way, we'll have to have a way for you to let me know right away and I will excuse you right away.

With a prearranged signal, like scratching her nose, Betsy will make her mother aware of her discomfort and she'll be excused as soon as introductions are over. Betsy feels relieved and grateful that her mother will recognize her uneasiness and respond to it in the future. It leaves Betsy with an impression of her own worth, sure of what she felt, and free to react to it. She is validated by Jean's acceptance of her discomfort and her respect for her feelings.

Often, several values clash in a single incident; in this case, good manners, honesty, trust, and self-worth. While we want our children to be polite, we want them to be honest, too. We need not choose one value over others. It's just a matter of how to handle them in the child's best interest.

Betsy's intuition was working. Her uncomfortable feeling may one day save her from becoming involved in an abusive relationship or from being manipulated by con artists or cult recruiters or, worse still, anyone with intent to harm her. Indeed, her strong intuitive reaction may one day save her life. In the aftermath, Jean and Tim discuss the matter:

Tim: Did you punish her?

Jean: No.

Tim: Well, did you tell her how embarrassed we were?

Jean: Actually, I dealt with *her* feelings instead of ours.

Tim: But does she understand what she did? Does she realize she made a bad impression on my boss's wife and what it could mean?

Jean: I doubt that your job depends upon the behavior of a five-year-old child. Anyway, Betsy had a strong intuitive feeling and she acted on it. I think we ought to respect and encourage that, not punish her for it.

Tim: Maybe the feeling was just indigestion and it had nothing to do with Mrs. Bluefeather.

Jean: The only way she'll ever know the difference between her intuition and indigestion is through her own experience. If we tell her that her negative feelings are wrong, she'll never know the difference and what's worse, she'll never learn to trust her intuition. Sure, she'll be wrong some of the time, but isn't it better for her to be wrong some of the time than to squelch her intuition altogether?

Tim: Are you saying it is okay for her to be rude?

Jean: Not at all, but we were so concerned about making a good impression that we never considered Betsy's genuine feelings. Besides, I think we made a mistake as well. We can't dictate or predict how she should feel about people. She has a right to her feelings, whatever they are. Anyway, Betsy and I worked out a way for her to signal me to excuse her if this should happen again.

Tim: I think you're right.

In today's world, it is imperative that we strengthen and support our children's intuitive feelings. Instead of frightening them about strangers, we need to build their intuition and trust in themselves. Think how confusing it must be to a small child who has been taught that she must not talk to strangers, and then when a friendly stranger on an elevator says, "Hello," we coax her to be polite and say, "Hello." I am of the opinion that it is a good idea for children to respond to as many strangers as possible, *in your presence only and followed up with your helping your child identify his and her feelings,* so that they experience and understand their different reactions to people. In this way, they will strengthen their intuition by being able to tell the difference between the feelings they get from the good guys and from the bad.

Your acceptance of your child's feelings is crucial to the development of his or her self-esteem and intuition.

Understand the Adolescent

Self-discovery is the work of adolescents. Their need to establish their identity spurs them to separate from their parents in every way. The urge to individuate sends them seeking answers to essential questions: *Who am I? What do I think? What do I believe? What do I feel apart from my parents' influence?* They want to sift out what is uniquely theirs from what has been given to them or what some feel has been forced upon them. Adolescence is a crisis of identity from minute to minute.

Several parents echoed the words of one unhappy mother who said, "My daughter was the perfect child until she turned thirteen, and then, suddenly, she was a stranger." Emerging from childhood, adolescents are in an expansive time—a time to test and try out what this "in-between" period has to offer. They experiment. They want to find out where they belong, what suits them, what feels right for them. Adventures with their looks take them to such outlandish styles that parents want to go into hiding until the phase blows over. Some teenagers who follow trends among movie and rock stars may go to extremes in their dress as well as their lifestyles. Some even want to try on new moralities in an effort to test the validity of their family values. However, after having worked with families for nearly half a century and observed them as they contended with the ups and downs of life with teenagers, it seems to me that young people who have been respected throughout their childhood have less need to go overboard in their experimentation.

Preadolescence

The problems of adolescence can be a beacon for parents of small children. By looking ahead, they can get an early start on preventing whatever problems are predictably preventable. A lot depends on what preceded the turbulent time of adolescence. The respected child is more likely to be respectful at adolescence. The child who has handled a good measure of autonomy all along is better prepared to deal with freedom and the new responsibilities adolescence brings—driving, dating, curfews, choice of friends, clothing styles, and the like. This period disrupts even the most stable families, and it is as hard on the teenagers as it is on their parents. In my outreach group for at-risk teenagers, every one of them said they wished they got along better with their parents. No child wants a bad relationship with his or her parents. Teenagers just don't know how to balance their struggle for independence with the guidance their parents still offer.

Some parents in our groups thought that strict control in the early years would guarantee their children's self-control when they reached adolescence. These parents were surprised when it didn't turn out that way. Self-control at adolescence comes from all the previous years of practicing control of their impulses, from learning to delay gratification, from learning the consequences of their behavior, from taking responsibility for their choices, and from understanding how their choices affect their own lives and the lives of others.

"Don't you trust me?" asks the teenager who wants the freedom to make his own choices. But what if he hasn't learned self-control as he was growing up? On what basis can his parents trust him? If he has earned his parents' trust throughout childhood by delivering on his promises and exhibiting integrity and honesty, they feel they can trust him. With that background, they can expect him to exercise self-control, to make his own healthy decisions, and handle freedom responsibly.

When our children are young and we feel so close to them, we can't imagine that one day they could disconnect and distance themselves from us. The mother who said her daughter was the perfect child until she turned thirteen and then was "suddenly a stranger" raises questions for all of us. When pressed to explain what she meant by "perfect," she said that Kathy was "an obedient child" who never gave her "a moment's trouble." When we asked her to explain why she called Kathy a "stranger," she said, "She started to think for herself."

Children can and should think for themselves long before they are thirteen. They don't get a sudden attack of adolescence and turn against their parents. The years before adolescence and children's relationships during that time will influence the extent of their teenage rebellion. Therefore, let's consider childhood as the time to lay the groundwork for lasting closeness and loyalty.

Emerging Autonomy

Adolescence is a normal and necessary breaking-away time, but it need not be a time when relationships break down. Though we wonder and worry how far our children will stray from family values and standards in their experimentation, we can hold ourselves and our families together by having faith in the strength of our relationships. It may seem that our children have no use for us during adolescence. Quite to the contrary, they don't want us to abandon them no matter how difficult or strange their behavior.

Some of the youngsters in my outreach group were drug abusers. Their relationships with their parents were strained to the breaking point. One night, I invited a drug abuse counselor to one of our meetings. She showed a film in which a father discovered that his teenage son was using drugs. After his initial shock, he took his son on a camping trip to reconnect with him. When the boy tried to run away, his father chased after him, caught him, held him close, and said, "I will not let you go." At that moment, the boy in the film seemed reassured and safe. But at that same moment, all the young people in the group turned away. They had lost all hope that their fathers would find a way back to them and hold on to them.

Adolescents are a mass of contradictions, and trying to cope with their sudden mood swings can be maddening. In their effort to establish their identity, they need space. They test out new ideas, even when they know their parents will object. New experiences help them sort out their own values. Parents are still important to them, though it often doesn't appear that way. Because their reliance on our support shifts to their peers, they can't hear us when we insist that they "be individuals" and not follow the crowd. Their overriding need is to fit in with their group. We must have faith that our relationship with them will see us through while they try out their new ideas and actions. A respected child will become a self-respecting teenager, one who is apt to take seriously the consequences of her decisions and actions and who will be more open to consider our point of view.

Adolescents often change their minds as they try to figure out their own style, their friends, their values, and their life-long goals. Some depart from childhood and parental ties reluctantly, while others, ready or not, rush headlong into adult behaviors. They try to bring together into a comprehensible whole what they hear and feel and what they perceive through their own experiences and needs—which now includes their sexuality.

We can avoid feeling rejected by our adolescents' lack of consideration for us when we realize what is happening to them during this tumultuous time. Of course, they don't say so, but they do appreciate the limits we set for them. With a little bit of luck, and a history of respect, they will trust that the limits we set are signs of our love and concern. Without mutual respect and trust, however, they misconstrue limits as an attempt to control them. That brings out their staunchest defiance. It is crucial to our mental health, and to theirs, to understand their defenses and to tune in to their feelings and their meanings. If ever it was necessary to listen with the heart, it is now.

The Need to Belong

This period puts enormous stress on every member of the family. The appeal and pressure of peers is heavy and hard to resist. The need for acceptance lures some adolescents into costly and dangerous experimentation. The problems of youth are astounding. The estimates of people of all ages who have become involved in destructive cults at one time or another range from 3 million to as many as 10 million.

The negative aspects of cults and gangs, of teen pregnancies, and of runaways prevent us from seeing that these groups and activities meet real needs. When a group of teenage girls were asked why they wanted to get pregnant, they said they wanted someone of their own to love. They were willing to trade in their youth for it. We think they are merely shortsighted and assume that if we can make them see what parenthood entails they would not consider it at such an early age. But this rational view overlooks a need so powerful it can neither wait nor be dissuaded. At any age, girls engage in sexual activity to feel loved, or at least wanted, even if only for the moment. Or they believe it will make them popular. How can we prevent a longing for the kind of love that young girls think only a baby or casual sex can fulfill? Strengthening our families will do it. Children who feel safe and secure, loved and respected in their families, will not need to manufacture another family or forfeit their freedom for a baby or a one-night stand.

Street gangs become families. Cults become families. In the drug culture and among runaways, street people bond as families. What can we learn from these groups? What does this tell us about their needs and the needs of our own children? We know these substitute families provide support, a sense of belonging, acceptance, security, a feeling of fellowship, and loyalty. In return, the lost and the lonely give their groups complete devotion. No matter how difficult some periods of life with children may be, we must never underestimate the power of family ties. The alienated youngsters I knew never stopped hungering for a relationship with their parents. I believe that broken relationships can be healed, that mutual forgiveness is possible, and that reconciliation is achievable when parents and children commit themselves to their relationships. I have seen this occur in hundreds of families.

When I was the director of a cult-education and resource center, parents came for help in reestablishing communication with their cult-involved adult sons and daughters. Here we had families and relationships torn apart by powerful forces. In cults, new members were pressured by peers to conform to a new lifestyle and belief system, cult leaders became new parent figures, and the group became a new family. Having lost all contact with their children for long periods of time, parents were filled with pain and fear and hopelessness. Yet, by learning how to have an honest discourse with their children, they were able to establish new relationships—for some, even better than the ones they'd had before. The parents dedicated themselves to making the relationship their top priority. It is never too late.

The key to healing broken relationships is the parents' willingness to set aside their personal disappointments, fears, and needs and reach out to their children from a locus of love.

The How-Can-I-Get-My-Teenager-to-Do-What-He-Has-to-Do Blues

When something stalls a capable adolescent from academic achievement, your nagging, scolding, punishing, bribing, humiliating, embarrassing, or even trying to reason with him probably won't work. "You don't care about *me*! All you care about are my grades so you can tell all your friends what a smart kid you have," complained one nagged, scolded, punished, and humiliated high school senior. Doreen remained unconvinced when her parents said they nagged out of love and concern for her. She felt cut off from them when they focused on the grades she brought home. She needed them to realize that she had reasons for her poor performance.

By now you have seen how many different areas of parenting success depend on knowing your child. If you have come to know him, then you will know what approach will work best and what words he is most likely to respond to in a positive way. The words you use, the feelings you have, and how you look at your child when you discuss the touchy issue of schoolwork will certainly affect the outcome. Taking your child's sensitivities into consideration will prevent him from construing your effort to motivate him as disapproval and personal rejection. For example, when a parent says angrily, "Why don't you study?" the child, feeling attacked, hears, "Why *won't* you study?" He can't see, or appreciate, that his parent is trying to help him. What he feels is that he is being accused of *deliberately* shirking his responsibility. So what was meant to motivate humiliates instead. He digs in his heels and makes excuses for himself. He'll save face by appearing not to care. And his parents take it literally and personally.

Many parents are stumped when their capable children do not strive to achieve. If your child is stalled in his school performance, if he has a low level of energy or attention, if he seems disinterested in the world around him, he needs help. These are

183

not deliberate behaviors but may be symptoms of a problem he does not know how to handle. A complete medical exam would rule out physical problems and hearing and vision problems as well. Simply labeling a child "lazy" does little good and only serves to make adversaries of parent and child. School guidance counselors and mental health professionals have the tools to help children discover what is blocking them. They can offer children constructive coping skills and help them move forward with their lives. I highly recommend any book written by Dr. Mel Levine, but for the problem of underachieving in particular, *The Myth of Laziness* offers excellent help and insight.

Lou said he was stumped and desperate for help. He claimed he had "tried everything" to get his son, Henry, to stop "goofing off." Instead of studying, this bright fifteen-year-old was playing video games for hours and, then, at the last minute, he crammed for tests. Most of the time he failed or just barely passed. First, Lou pleaded, then he bribed, then he threatened, and finally he punished Henry, without getting the results he wanted. We had the following conversation:

> *Lou:* I just can't understand how he can be so stupid! He says he wants to go to college and yet he spends hours playing video games. College? I told him at this rate he'll never get out of high school!
>
> *Me:* And what was his response?
>
> *Lou:* He said he was bored with school.
>
> *Me:* And what do you make of that?
>
> *Lou:* It's just a good excuse to goof off.
>
> *Me:* How does he think you should be dealing with this?
>
> *Lou:* He says I should leave him alone.
>
> *Me:* Could you do that?
>
> *Lou:* If I leave him alone, he'll never do anything but play those games.
>
> *Me:* And then what will happen?
>
> *Lou:* Then he'll never get to college.

Me: You know, Lou, not everyone was meant for college.

Lou: So then I'll wind up stuck with him for the rest of my life?

Lou saw only two possibilities—his son would go to college or he'd be stuck forever with a game-playing ne'er-do-well. Some young people bloom late. They are in a quandary as to what they want to do with their lives and cannot conceive of making decisions about it when they are fifteen. With no clear vision of a career, many find school boring and the subjects without relevance to "real life." Henry toyed with the idea of becoming a lawyer, but he saw no connection between his current behavior and the demands of law school. Something is blocking Henry.

There was a time in America when not every child was expected to go to college. Nor did every child have any interest in furthering his education beyond high school. Before the Russians launched *Sputnik* and beat America in the race to outer space, it was mostly gifted or privileged individuals who went to college. In the twenty-first century, however, young people have less of a chance to advance in the marketplace with only a high school education. We parents need to do everything we can to foster our children's development, interests, and abilities.

Give your child the benefit of the doubt. If she has succeeded in the past and does not have a physical blockage that accounts for her low school performance, trust that she has a reason that needs your understanding and help.

SECRET 25

❧

Communicate

The word *communicate* means to impart, bestow, or convey; to make known; to give by way of information. If words were all we needed to communicate no mother would ever have to say "how many times do I have to tell you . . . " or "I've told you a million times . . . " In the best of all worlds, in which words had such power, our children would hear our words the first and only time and they'd do as they were told. Forever.

Pam (barging into her teenage son's room): Clean your room! It looks like a pig sty!

What has Jeff's mother imparted, conveyed, made known?

Jeff: It's my room. If you don't like it, don't come in!

What has Jeff imparted, conveyed, made known? "Clean your room" is clear. Why isn't Jeff getting Pam's message? And why isn't she getting his? If communication is the key to successful relationships and words don't work, what will?

We know that communication begins with listening. But, we insist, we *do* listen. Yet what do we hear? Can Jeff know what feelings lie beneath Pam's words? What meaning does Pam give to Jeff's words? What feelings did Pam's words evoke in her son? What feelings did Jeff's words tap in his mother?

Pam's disappointment stems from another definition of the word *communicate:* to share in common, to participate with. Isn't this the essence of what parents hope for? Don't we want to share in common with our children our cherished values and participate in a life of mutual caring? We can, in fact, make it happen. Let's take another look at what Pam said, how she said it, what she really meant, and what Jeff heard.

Pam said: Clean your room! It looks like a pig sty!
She means: *The mess in this room really upsets me and I worry about your sense of responsibility* [Futurethink].
Jeff heard: *The room is more important to me than you are.*

She feels: Disappointment, fear, resentment, concern.
He feels: Resentment, humiliation, hurt.
She conveyed: Anger
Message he got: *I'm never good enough.*

She thought she was teaching: Responsibility
He learned: To keep his door locked.

Neither Pam nor Jeff conveyed their true thoughts and feelings. Pam's angry words did not get across the disappointment and sadness she feels because she and her son do not share common values of orderliness and cleanliness. She wonders whether he will reject all the other values she has tried to teach him. She is concerned for his future, fearing that today's messy room means he will *never* assume responsibility for his life.

Then doubt sets in about the job she has done as a parent. She wonders if he's deliberately untidy, just to get even with her, and if so, what has she done do to deserve this? *Is he rejecting me?* And resentment. *Even if he doesn't want to do it for himself, why can't he do it as a consideration for me?* All this was triggered by the sight of the room. Her order to clean his room only hinted at the knot of fears and feelings she harbored.

Jeff is sixteen years old. He drives a car he paid for himself, he has a part-time job, he's a computer whiz, he has sound plans for his future, and he is sexually active. His worries range from getting good grades to getting into a good college to getting a pimple on his face the night of the prom. He fears AIDS, drugs, crime, and nuclear war. He feels he is on the brink of adulthood and he wants to be treated accordingly. He wants the right to make his own decisions, including how he keeps his room. He bristles at his mother's commanding tone of voice—the same one he heard when he was a little boy. The room symbolizes the distance between them. Jeff is angry and hurt, believing as he does that the condition of the room means more to his mother than he does. It is his private domain and he resents her barging in.

How can Pam and Jeff become participants in a life of mutual caring? What will it take for each to be open to the other and to tune in to the other's underlying meanings?

Let's try respect:

Pam (knocking on her son's bedroom door): May I come in, Jeff?
Jeff: Sure, Mom, but brace yourself, my room's a mess.
Pam: I know you're studying for finals, so you don't have a lot of time these days.
Jeff: I'll straighten up before I go to bed.
Pam: Would you like some help?
Jeff: Thanks, Mom, but no, I can handle it.

Pam's respect for Jeff began with a knock on the door. His respect for her began with his fair warning of what to expect, taking away the shock effect of what lays before her. Pam gives Jeff the benefit of the doubt as to why he has not cleaned the room; she doesn't pinch his defenses by attacking him. He, on the other hand, knows how his mother feels about tidiness so he forewarns her before she opens the door. He also indicates that he cares about it, too. Here is what they communicated to each other this time:

She said (after knocking): May I come in?
He feels: *She respects me.*
She said: I know you are studying.
He feels: *She understands the pressure I'm under.*
She said: Would you like some help?
He feels: *She cares about* me.
He said: Brace yourself . . .
She feels: *He knows what I care about.*
He said: I'll straighten up . . .
She feels: *He is responsible.*
He feels: *She really cares about me.*

But suppose Jeff's room is always messy? If Jeff has not learned by now to keep an orderly room, screaming at him at this point won't change his long-standing behavior. Some children seem to be born with a natural propensity for orderliness and for others, it is a struggle. And some youngsters simply don't care about it at any age. Orderliness needs to be cultivated early in children who are not naturally endowed with a sense of it. They need a lot of help and encouragement when they are young. Extra cubby-holes, bookshelves, drawers, hooks, hampers, and pegboards can modify the chaos. Like any other skill, they need to learn how to organize. It also helps to have neat but not fanatical parents. Some children, along with their parents, have the ability to live in the middle of a disaster area and not notice it at all. Others get depressed in such a setting and appreciate help in getting it straightened up. Sometimes a messy room reflects how the child feels about himself. In that case it is the child's inner turmoil, not the room, that needs special attention.

Words, Words, Words

If people could alter their behavior with words alone, prevention messages would succeed in stopping all self-destructive habits. We could *just tell* people to stop overeating, smoking, abusing drugs and alcohol, and their problems would be over. Although some people can respond to dire warnings automatically, from the looks of it, many cannot. For them, it takes more than words to bring about change and effective communication. We may hear all the good words, agree with them, love their message, *know* exactly what we must do to change, and still not be able to act on it.

Minds don't function apart from feelings. In fact, our emotions dictate most decisions and many fly in the face of reason. How often do you hear people say, "I *know* I shouldn't, but. . . ." Just knowing the consequences of unhealthy habits is not enough to make us change. In fact, the facts themselves can create enough anxiety to keep a person locked into a bad habit.

It isn't true that the longer the monologue, the more impressed the child will be. Here's a charming true story about too many words, told to me by a psychologist friend.

The minute Pete came through his front door, he could see his wife was having a bad day. Looking frazzled and exhausted, she pushed their three-year-old daughter, Joy, toward him and said, "Here, you talk to her. Maybe she'll listen to you."

Standing confidently behind his Ph.D. in child psychology, Pete escorted the little girl into her bedroom, closed the door, then sat down on the bed next to her for a chat. He began by telling her how families are a team, how they are supposed to work together, respect each other, care about each other, and always listen when someone is speaking.

On and on and on he droned. After a few minutes, Pete paused and waited for Joy's response. More minutes passed and finally Pete asked, "Well, young lady, what do you have to say for yourself?"

The glassy-eyed child yawned and wearily replied, "Sing me another song, Daddy."

Communication is more than merely using words—it includes the way you look when you speak, the voice and tone you use, the feelings that lie beneath your words, the words you choose, the timing of your words, the attitude with which you deliver your words, the meanings of your words, the meanings your child gives to your words. Children resist words that lack respect. And words, kind or cruel, last a lifetime.

Close the Generation Gap

Changes in moral values have widened the gulf between the generations in many families. Parents find it hard to cope with modern trends in music, films, books, language, sexual mores, and dress, let alone accept them. Even the baby boomers who defied convention in their youth, now parents themselves, cannot comprehend the extremes to which today's young people have gone. How can we talk to our sons and daughters about the danger of sexually transmitted diseases, unwanted pregnancy, and AIDS so that they hear us? How can we understand their ideas when they are so different from our own? How do we fit into their lives when they live in a world so foreign to us? How can we guide our children to make healthy choices when their peers engage in destructive behavior?

The stresses on today's parents are enormous, especially in regard to the health and safety of their children. Young people are bombarded with titillating sexual images on television and movie screens and by the explicit language they hear in their music. With all these influences bearing down on them, parents fear that their values and standards will be forsaken. In the following scenario, Lila comes face to face with a moment she never anticipated with her fifteen-year-old daughter.

Tina: I was thinking about getting birth control pills.
Lila: Over my dead body!
Tina: Mother! Get real! This is the twenty-first century.
Lila: I don't care what century it is, you are not getting birth control pills at the age of fifteen. The very thought of it makes me sick.

Lila hoped her strong reaction would put an end to Tina's intention, not only of getting birth control pills but also of engaging in sexual activity. It was the last-ditch effort of a frightened parent to impart values, but Tina saw it only as her mother's attempt to control her. Did Lila's reaction have the effect she desired? To the contrary, it raised her daughter's defenses, so instead of serving as a deterrent, it risked propelling Tina into making a reactive choice. She feels she is on the brink of womanhood, yet her mother is still treating her like a child. Lila's strong, off-putting reaction could push Tina to seek comfort from her boyfriend, spurring her to engage in sex with him just to prove her "maturity." Lila could not foresee this possibility. She is single-minded of purpose. No birth control pill. No sex.

Let's see how a more respectful approach changes this scenario.

Tina: I want to get birth control pills.
Lila: Look, Tina, this subject needs more time and attention than I can give it right now. Let's discuss this after dinner when there won't be any distractions.

Alone in the kitchen as she prepares dinner, Lila's mind is racing with a torrent of fears and feelings about all the possibilities associated with her daughter's request. She is disappointed by her daughter's rejection of the family's moral and religious values. She feels uneasy about dealing with Tina's emerging womanhood. Her own aging and questions about her own sexuality rise to the surface. Lila realizes that she needs to separate all of these issues from her daughter's. She has heard the clarion call, "This is not about *you*, Mother." After dinner, Lila and Tina sit together in Tina's bedroom.

Lila: Okay, Tina, I'm listening.
Tina: Well, all my friends are on the pill.
Lila: Is that why you want it?
Tina: No, but Danny wants me to.
Lila: And how do *you* feel about it?
Tina: I don't know. I'm really confused.
Lila: About?
Tina: Sex.
Lila: What's confusing you?
Tina: Mom, when you love somebody shouldn't you love them completely?
Lila: Maybe we ought to talk about this before we discuss the pill. What do you think?
Tina: I don't know what to think. A lot of my friends are having sex with their boyfriends, but then when they break up, some of the girls said they feel awful about the sex part.
Lila: What do they mean by "awful?"
Tina: Well, they say they feel "used."
Lila: Why would they feel "used"?
Tina: That's the part I don't understand. I asked them and they don't seem to know, except that some guys dump them right after they've had sex—like they're not interested in them anymore. So how do I know Danny won't dump me?
Lila: Does that make you question your relationship with him?
Tina: I haven't thought about that. Anyway, Danny says that if I love him I'll show it by having sex with him.
Lila: And what do you think?
Tina: I just don't know. Kids much younger than me are having sex parties with guys they don't even know. They

even do it in groups. So I don't know what the big deal is. Then I wonder where love comes in. I thought sex was part of love.

Lila: People have sex without love and others have love without sex, Tina. I don't think the little girls you're talking about have any idea about the consequences of what they are doing.

Tina: Like what?

Lila: Like discovering that they *are* being used as your friends feel. Nor do they understand the health risks involved. Do you also feel pressured to have sex because your friends are sexually active or that if "everyone is doing it," that it is all right to do?

Tina: Sort of, and, well, Danny is pressuring me.

Lila: How do you feel about that?

Tina: I don't think he ought to pressure me about it.

Lila: How do you handle it when he does?

Tina: I just tell him I'm not ready, which has just been an excuse, but now I think it's true. I don't think I am *really* ready. There's a lot more I need to know.

Lila: That's true. For example, do you know that starting on the pill at an early age could cause physical complications later? That's what I read, but look, this is too serious an issue for us to guess about. I think it would be a good idea for you to talk it over with Dr. Gordon. And while you're at it, you might want to discuss some other things.

Tina: Like what?

Lila: A lot is at stake when you become sexually active. The pill won't protect you from getting AIDS or the other STDs.

Tina: I hadn't thought about that, either.

Lila: How about pregnancy? If you should forget to take the pill . . . Look, you know by now that your father and I regard abstinence as the only safe way. Now it turns out

we're not the only ones who think this way. AIDS educa-
tors and doctors are saying it, too.

Tina: I guess you're right about having a lot of things to
think about.

How did Tina feel after this discussion? *Mom was willing to listen
to me. I know she has very strong feelings about this, but she was willing
to hear me out. She was really interested in what I think and feel. She
wants me to have good information instead of just guessing. She gave
me important questions to think about. She trusts me to think things
through. And she didn't condemn my friends or Danny. I can talk to her
about anything. She really knows how to help me. She respects me.*
What a good talk! By not letting her judgments and personal
feelings dominate, Lila was able to raise important and potentially
lifesaving issues. At the same time she learned how much Tina
knew and still needed to know. She gave her daughter a broader
range of matters to think about. She recommended a visit to the
doctor for his advice on the use of pills and prevention of disease.
Her calm demeanor enabled her daughter to reflect on her decision. Lila did not try to persuade Tina to accept her point of view,
though she mentioned it.

Teenage boys also need opportunities to deal with their feelings and thoughts about their sexuality. They, too, need solid information to counteract the influence of television and movie
images, locker-room banter, and their raging hormones.

What should we do when we are opposed to our child's choice
or decision? We have every right and the responsibility to warn
our children of the consequences. Where health is concerned,
we must do all we can to encourage our children to reconsider
their decisions in the light of sound medical information.

After reading this dialogue in a group, one mother asked about
Lila's initial "honest" reaction when she blurted out, "Over my
dead body." Wasn't she just being spontaneous and honest? Yes,
but sometimes what appears to be a forthright and honest response can be a reaction to something else, as Charley's mother

showed us. In the first scenario, the request for the birth control pill triggered Lila's deep-seated feelings. They spilled out in a single sentence. Parents need to be clear about their own sexuality before they can contend with their children's maturing needs. Many parents found it too difficult to deal with these matters with their children. I recommended that they find a family member or the family physician, a nurse, or a school guidance counselor to provide the kind of information their adolescents needed to make informed choices.

The sexual freedoms unleashed in the 1960s have continued to this day, filtering down to very young children, leaving today's parents in a state of shock. While we can acknowledge that our children are living in a very different time and place from the one we grew up in, we find it hard to deal with. We want to keep up with the times but we don't want to relinquish the values we cherish. Sometimes children find themselves caught between the values they learned in their families and opposing values outside their homes. A respectful and loving relationship with children is the best defense against the crude version of sexuality portrayed in movies and television.

Sexuality is not just a matter of physical sex. A healthy attitude toward sexuality derives from healthy relationships. It is influenced by wholesome relationships between the parents, between fathers and sons, mothers and daughters, fathers and daughters, and mothers and sons. Warm, affectionate, respectful relationships between parents provide a sound foundation for children's sexuality. As with all our values, the best way to communicate them is by living them. If your children see that your values have enhanced your life, and brought you joy and fulfillment, they are more likely to consider them for their own lives.

A FINAL SECRET

Believe in Yourself

Only connect.

E. M. Forster

Mutual respect connects us one to another for a lifetime. It prevents the natural drift at adolescence from becoming a permanent rift. Respect is the firm foundation for parents and children to remain significant persons in each other's lives. All of us, parents and children alike, want to feel connected; we want to belong. It happens after we have taken down the barriers that separate us: the phantoms of the past, our judgments, overreactions, fears, literal responses, and excessive sentimentality. Compassion connects us one to the other at a profound and spiritual level. It makes us feel safe in the other person's presence—safe from criticism, safe from judgments, safe from harm. We can count on the compassionate person to comfort and understand us, accept and love us just for who we are. How will you know that you have connected with your child in a healthy and meaningful way? You'll know when the feeling of connectedness lasts long after the words were uttered and the actions bonded you together. Those moments are riveted in the heart even when memory fails. Communication is a *meeting of meanings*. It happens when people wholly affirm one another. It begins with respect and ends with respect.

So now you know what it takes to raise amazing children—humility and patience, kindness and compassion, love and trust and respect. It takes a spirit free enough to accept your children *as* they are, for *who* they are—the sacred souls *that* they are. Raising amazing children takes parents who are willing to be amazing themselves. *You* can do it by reaching higher than you ever thought you could and by reaching deeper within yourself than you've ever done before—to bring out the very best that is in your child. By using the very best that is within you, you will discover that it was all there just waiting to unfold. *Indeed, the secrets were within you from the start.*

Let this be a beginning, not the end.

I would love to hear from you. If you have experiences to share, or feedback on using the secrets in this book, please email me at Molly@sidran.org.

Books to Inform and Inspire

Baum, Joanne. *Respectful Parenting*. Washington, DC: Child and Family Press, 2001. Softcover, 178 pages.

Bettelheim, Bruno. *A Good Enough Parent*. New York: Vintage Books/Random House, 1988. Softcover, 375 pages. Quotations at 78 and 85.

Elgin, Suzette Haden. *The Gentle Art of Communicating with Kids*. New York: John Wiley & Sons, 1996. Softcover, 179 pages.

Faber, Adele, and Elaine Mazlish. *How to Talk So Kids Will Listen and Listen So Kids Will Talk*. New York: Avon Books, 1980. Softcover, 233 pages.

Fromm, Erich. *The Art of Loving*. New York: Harper Perennial, 2000. Softcover, 144 pages.

Guarendi, Raymond N., with David Eich. *Back to the Family: Proven Advice on Building a Stronger, Healthier, Happier Family*. New York: Fireside Books, 1991. Softcover, 272 pages.

Hendrix, Harville, and Helen Hunt. *Giving the Love That Heals: A Guide for Parents*. New York: Pocket Books/Simon & Schuster, 1977/1997. Softcover, 345 pages.

Hertz, J. H., ed. *The Pentateuch and Haftorahs*. 2nd ed. London: Soncino Press, 1960. Quotation at 820.

Ilg, Frances L., Louise Bates Ames, and Sidney M. Baker. *The Classic Childcare Manual from the Gesell Institute of Human Development* New York: Harper Paperback, 1992. Softcover, 368 pages.

Jaska, Peter. *Twenty-five Stupid Mistakes Parents Make.* Chicago: Lowell House/NTC/Contemporary Publishing, 1998. Softcover, 226 pages.

Kohn, Alfie. *Unconditional Parenting.* New York: Atria Books, 2005. Hardcover, 221 pages.

Lieberman, Alicia. *Emotional Life of the Toddler.* New York: Free Press / Simon & Schuster, 1993. Softcover, 244 pages.

Nelsen, Jane, Lynn Lott, and H. Stephen Glenn. *Positive Discipline A–Z: 1001 Solutions to Everyday Parenting Problems.* Rockin, CA: Prima Publishing, 1999. Softcover, 317 pages.

Pieper, Martha Heineman, and William J. Pieper. *Smart Love: The Compassionate Alternative to Discipline That Will Make You a Better Parent and Your Child a Better Person.* Boston: Harvard Common Press, 1999. Softcover, 234 pages.

Rolfe, Randy. *The Seven Secrets of Successful Parents.* Chicago: Contemporary Books, 1998. Softcover, 273 pages.

Sears, Martha, and William Sears. *The Discipline Book: How to Have a Better Behaved Child from Birth to Age Ten.* Boston: Little, Brown & Co., 2003. Softcover, 328.

Spock, Benjamin, and Michael B. Rothenberg. *Dr. Spock's Baby and Child Care.* New York: Simon & Schuster, 1985. Softcover, 701 pages.

Steede, Kevin. *Ten Most Common Mistakes Good Parents Make (and How to Avoid Them).* Rocklin, CA: Prima Publishing, 1998. Softcover, 174 pages.

Steinberg, Laurence. *The Ten Basic Principles of Good Parenting.* New York: Simon & Schuster, 2004. Hardcover, 224 pages.

About
Sidran Institute

Sidran Institute, a leader in traumatic stress education and resources, is a national nonprofit organization devoted to helping people understand, recover from, and treat traumatic stress and related issues. We teach survivors, family members, and service providers; we consult with agencies and governments; we publish books, training materials, and assessment tools; and provide informational resources to thousands of survivors and providers each year. Our education and advocacy promotes greater understanding of:

- The early recognition and treatment of trauma-related stress in children;
- The long-term effects of trauma on adults;
- The strategies leading to greatest success in self-help recovery for trauma survivors, and support by and for their families;
- The most successful clinical methods and practices for treatment of trauma victims;
- The public policy initiatives that respond best to the needs of trauma survivors.

Programs

SIDRAN'S RESOURCE CENTER AND HELP DESK provides information resources at no cost to callers and e-mailers from around the English-speaking world. The information includes: names of trauma-experienced therapists, traumatic stress organizations, educational books and materials, conferences, trainings, and treatment facilities.

SIDRAN SPEAKERS, TRAINING AND CONSULTATION SERVICES provide conference and keynote speakers, pre-designed and custom training, consultation, and technical assistance on all aspects of traumatic stress-related content, including:

- Public Education and Consultation to organizations, associations, and governmental agencies on a variety of trauma topics and public education strategies.
- Agency Training, including our popular *Risking Connection* program, on trauma-related topics such as Trauma Symptom Management, Self-Care for Helpers, The Relationship between Trauma and Dangerous Behavior, and others. We will be glad to customize presentations for the specific needs of your agency or organization.
- Survivor and Community Education programming including how to start and maintain effective peer support groups, community networking for trauma support, self-determination, successful selection of therapists, coping skills, and healing skills.

SIDRAN INSTITUTE PRESS publishes books and educational materials on traumatic stress and dissociative conditions. A recently published example is *Risking Connection in Faith Communities: A Book for Faith Leaders Supporting Trauma Survivors.* Some of our other titles include *Growing Beyond Survival: A Self-Help Toolkit for Managing Traumatic Stress,* and *Back from the Front: Combat Trauma, Love, and the Family.*

SIDRAN PILOTS COLLABORATIVE PROJECTS that create integrated service systems for holistic support of trauma survivors. Sidran is proud of its record of collaboration with a diverse range of organizations.

For more information on any of these programs and projects, please contact us:

Sidran Institute
200 East Joppa Road, Suite 207, Baltimore, MD 21286
Phone: 410-825-8888 • Fax: 410-337-0747
E-mail: info@sidran.org • Website: www.sidran.org

Other Books by
Sidran Institute Press

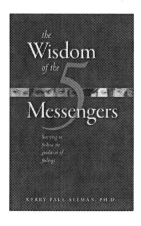

The Wisdom of the Five Messengers:
Learning to Follow the Guidance of
Feelings

Kerry Paul Altman, Ph.D.

"An original, readable, insightful book
that invites us to shift our attitudes about
emotions from sources of distress to clues
to self-healing and increased effectiveness."
—Adam Blatner, M.D., author of The Art of
Play: Helping Adults Reclaim Imagination &
Spontaneity

Back from the Front: Combat Trauma,
Love, and the Family

Aphrodite Matsakis, Ph.D.

". . . a superb resource that paves the way
to hope and healing for returning warriors,
their spouses, their families . . . and all
those who care about them."
—Lt. Colonel Dave Grossman,
U.S. Army, Ret.

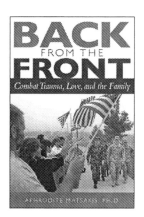

The Twenty-Four Carat Buddha and Other Fables: Stories of Self-Discovery

Maxine Harris, Ph.D.

"These thought-provoking tales are wonderful companions for the healing journey. Each story holds a nugget of truth—something precious to ponder and absorb."
—Laura Davis, author of *The Courage to Heal*

Restoring Hope and Trust:
An Illustrated Guide to Mastering Trauma

Lisa Lewis, Ph.D., Kay Kelly, MSW, LSCSW, and Jon Allen, Ph.D.

"In this modest but powerful book, persons struggling with the painful residue of trauma will find solace. . . ."
—Roy W. Menninger, M.D., Chairman Emeritus and Past President, Menninger

To read full descriptions of these and other books, please visit www.sidran.org.

Breinigsville, PA USA
28 October 2009
226668BV00002B/5/A